THIRD EDITION

Lower Secondary English 9

John Reynolds

The questions, example answers and comments that appear in this book were written by the author. In an examination, the way marks would be awarded to answers like these may be different.

Third-party websites and resources referred to in this publication have not been endorsed by Cambridge Assessment International Education.

Although every effort has been made to ensure that website addresses are correct at time of going to press, Hodder Education cannot be held responsible for the content of any website mentioned in this book. It is sometimes possible to find a relocated web page by typing in the address of the home page for a website in the URL window of your browser.

Hachette UK's policy is to use papers that are natural, renewable and recyclable products and made from wood grown in well-managed forests and other controlled sources. The logging and manufacturing processes are expected to conform to the environmental regulations of the country of origin.

Orders: please contact Hachette UK Distribution, Hely Hutchinson Centre, Milton Road, Didcot, Oxfordshire, OX11 7HH. Telephone: +44 (0)1235 827827. Email education@hachette.co.uk Lines are open from 9 a.m. to 5 p.m., Monday to Friday.

ISBN: 978 1 3983 0189 4

© John Reynolds 2022

First published in 2011

First published in 2022 by Hodder Education (a trading division of Hodder & Stoughton Limited),

An Hachette UK Company

Carmelite House

50 Victoria Embankment

London EC4Y 0DZ

www.hoddereducation.com

The authorised representative in the EEA is Hachette Ireland, 8 Castlecourt Centre, Dublin 15, D15 XTP3, Ireland (email: info@hbgi.ie)

Impression number 10 9 8 7 6 5

Year 2026 2025

All rights reserved. Apart from any use permitted under UK copyright law, no part of this publication may be reproduced or transmitted in any form or by any means, electronic or mechanical, including photocopying and recording, or held within any information storage and retrieval system, without permission in writing from the publisher or under licence from the Copyright Licensing Agency Limited. Further details of such licences (for reprographic reproduction) may be obtained from the Copyright Licensing Agency Limited, www.cla.co.uk

Cover photo © peangdao - stock.adobe.com

Illustrations by Oxford Designers and Illustrators and Abigael Cassell

Typeset by Ian Foulis Design, Saltash, Cornwall

Printed and bound in Great Britain by Bell and Bain Ltd, Glasgow

A catalogue record for this title is available from the British Library.

Contents

Introduction ... iv
How to use this book ... v
The reading cycle ... vii
The writing cycle ... ix

Chapter 1: Capturing the experience ... 1

Chapter 2: Remembering and informing ... 21

Chapter 3: Writing to persuade ... 41

Chapter 4: Painting pictures ... 59

Chapter 5: Advertising ... 77

Chapter 6: A good story ... 93

Chapter 7: Exploring complex themes ... 111

Chapter 8: Bringing it all together ... 129

Glossary ... 140
Acknowledgements ... 141

Cambridge Checkpoint Lower Secondary English

Introduction

Cambridge Checkpoint Lower Secondary English Student's Book 9 is the third in a series of three books designed to cover the Cambridge Lower Secondary English curriculum framework.

This Student's Book will build on the key skills and types of texts you met in Stages 7 and 8, building up your vocabulary, diving deeper into a range of texts and writers, and providing lots of opportunities to practise and consolidate your English skills through a range of group work and individual activities.

We hope the work you do in this book will be enjoyable and challenging, whether it sets you up for further study in English or provides valuable practice for your use of English in everyday situations.

You will cover a range of activities to practise your reading, writing, speaking and listening skills.

Each chapter also contains key skills sections which home in on a specific topic. Some of these may be revision activities, such as revisiting how to use punctuation for effect and varying sentence types, but some may introduce newer areas of learning, such as autobiographical poems and travel blogs. The texts and activities become more challenging as you work through each book to match your growing understanding of English.

You will find a variety of genres in the reading texts, drawn from a range of cultures, geographical locations and authorial voices. There should be something interesting here for everybody and you may find new styles of writing you haven't encountered before!

We hope you enjoy the exercises and activities in this book alongside your studies of Cambridge Lower Secondary English. Ask for help if you need it but try hard first. Studying English stretches and develops your skill set and it can be very rewarding!

How to use this book

The *chapter opener* pages give you a snapshot of all the exciting reading, writing, speaking and listening skills you will practise in the chapter, along with the key skill(s) you will focus on, and introduce the new topic with a discussion.

Activity

These boxes allow you to explore and practise skills in pairs or groups.

EXERCISE

These boxes allow you to practise and consolidate skills on your own and occasionally with a partner or group.

Author, poet or playwright

These boxes provide extra information about the creators of texts. This is often useful when a text has been created in a particular social, historical or political context.

KEY WORDS

These boxes explain all the literary and grammar terms. The key words are repeated in the glossary pages at the back of the book for easy revision.

LET'S TALK

These activities offer opportunities to discuss the content in pairs, groups or as a class.

Spotlight on
These boxes ask you to think about specific aspects of the text, such as purpose, audience, historical context and theme.

WORD ATTACK SKILLS
These boxes ask you to look at vocabulary and language in context. This includes working out the meaning of unfamiliar words, looking at a writer's choice of language and discussing linguistic and literary techniques.

HINT
These boxes guide you to think about specific things.

The *Reviewing* section at the end of each chapter lets you evaluate the texts you have read, suggests similar or contrasting texts for further reading and asks you to reflect on your learning in the chapter.

🔊 This means that there is a listening activity, with an audio track reference. All audio is available to download for free from www.hoddereducation.com/cambridgeextras

EXTENSION
These are more demanding tasks or tasks that help you to practise a wider range of skills.

GLOSSARY
This box gives you the meaning of any words from the text that may be new or challenging.

Do you remember?
Find a quick reminder about things you should already have learned in these features.

DID YOU KNOW?
Discover interesting facts in these boxes.

The reading cycle

Follow these three steps to read actively:

1 **Before reading**
It may sound silly to prepare your brain to read a text, but knowing what the text type or genre is and what subject you are reading about helps you to comprehend what you read and to make connections to past learning and/or experiences.
   - Look for clues about the text type or genre.
   - Read the title and subtitle to find out what the text is about.
   - Use skimming and scanning techniques to look for:
     - the layout of the text
     - heading levels and/or numbering of headings or subheadings
     - emphasis given through the use of different colours, key words, italics or bold
     - artwork, illustrations and/or photographs and their captions
     - graphics and graphs, diagrams, charts or maps
     - key words or specific details.

2 **During reading**
These activities will help you to analyse the structure and language features in more detail.
   - Use the Word attack skills boxes to work out the meaning of words using contextual clues, the word families they are from, the morphology or root of the words.
   - Ask questions while you read. Use the questions that appear alongside the texts.
   - Make notes of main and supporting ideas.
   - Visualise what is being described (particularly in descriptive writing).
   - Pay attention to the way the creator of the text has used language and grammar to enhance the meaning in texts and to create effects.

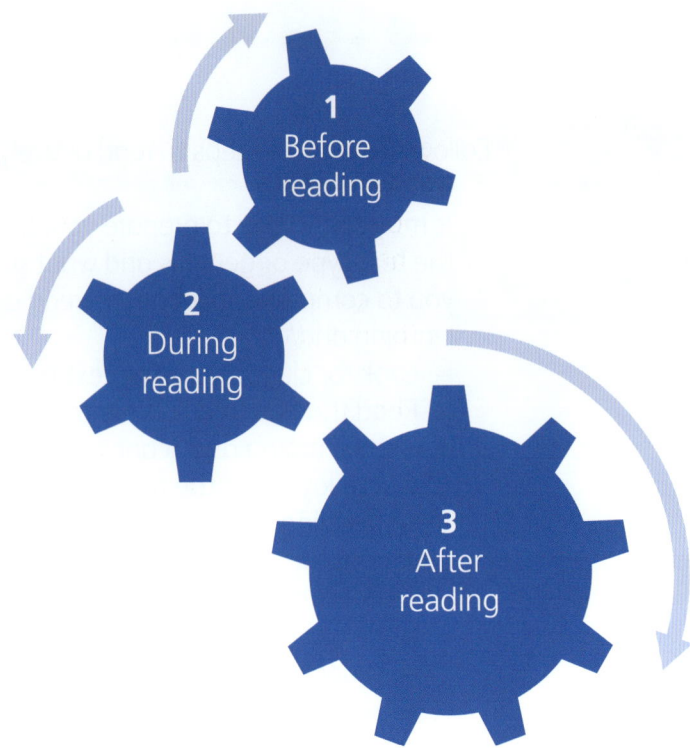

3. **After reading**
   These activities will help you to understand the meaning of the text.
   - Think about the purpose and audience of the text. What was it supposed to do? Who was it written for?
   - Evaluate the impact of the text on you. What is your opinion of the text?
   - Evaluate and discuss different interpretations of the text.
   - Think about texts that are similar to, or contrast with, the text.
   - Exercise critical language awareness:
     - Distinguish between facts and opinions.
     - Compare direct (explicit) and implied (implicit) information and meaning.
     - Determine the social, political and cultural background of texts.
     - Identify emotive and manipulative language such as stereotyping and bias.

Cambridge Checkpoint Lower Secondary English

The writing cycle

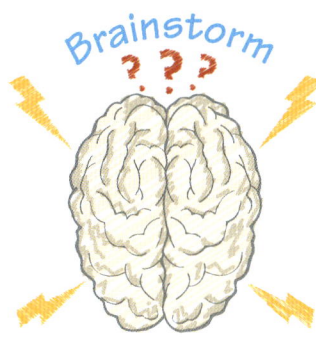

1 Generate ideas by brainstorming, writing your ideas on paper or talking with others or doing research. Think about:
   - your audience – who will read your work? Who is your text for?
   - the intended purpose of your writing – is it to entertain, inform, persuade or a combination of those things?
   - the writing features you will use to suit the text type or genre.
2 Organise your ideas by planning your writing.
   - Use different planning methods to shape your ideas, such as a mind map, a storyboard or an online template.

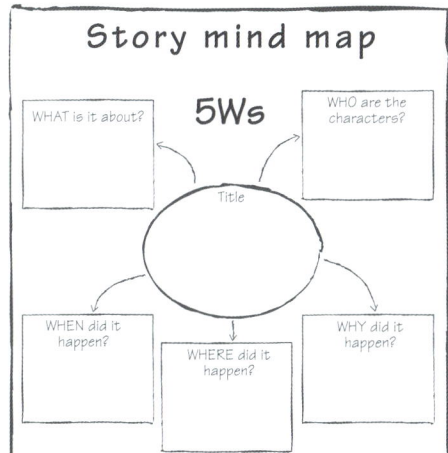

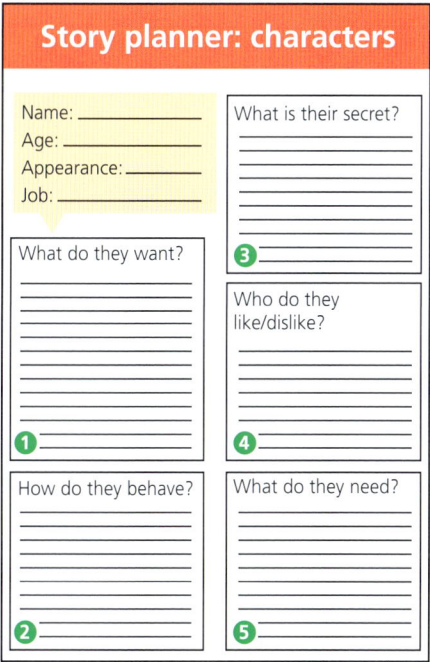

3 Write a draft. Think about:
 - the tone and register (formal or informal) you should use
 - the purpose
 - the intended audience.
4 Revise your draft. Think about:
 - the types of sentences you could use: simple, compound or complex sentences and using different types of sentences to avoid monotony
 - the range of punctuation you could use (pages 4–5)
 - how you can develop distinctive voices for your characters (pages 30–31)
 - the range of language you could use to make your writing more interesting, such as using better adjectives or adverbs (page 69).
5 Edit your writing.
 - Evaluate your writing by checking your language, grammar, spelling and the structure of your writing.
 - Ask a partner to read your writing and do the same.
 - Correct any mistakes.
6 Proofread your writing.
 - Rewrite or type your work. Think about different layouts and decide which one will best suit your purpose: handwritten, printed or onscreen.
 - Read through your work carefully to make sure that you have corrected all your mistakes.
7 Present your writing.

1 Capturing the experience

Reading
★ Travel blogs
★ Travel in the news
★ Emotive texts

Speaking and listening
★ Discussing purpose
★ Discussing humour and audience enjoyment
★ Listening to travel blogs

CAPTURING THE EXPERIENCE

Writing
★ A travel blog
★ Sensory writing
★ An analysis
★ Emotive writing
★ An account of a journey

Key skills
★ Literary devices such as euphemism, litotes, understatement and hyperbole
★ Using a visual organiser to plan writing
★ Using punctuation for effect

LET'S TALK
- Do you like to travel? Can you explain why or why not?
- Some people think of themselves as <u>travellers</u> rather than as tourists. Do you think there is a difference between a tourist and a traveller?
- Some people travel because it is necessary or required. Can you think of reasons why travel may be necessary?

1 CAPTURING THE EXPERIENCE

Reading and speaking

Different purposes ... different audiences

Journeys are popular subjects in both fiction and non-fiction. Fiction often features fantasy travel adventures, in which people set off on quests to find objects, or to find the meaning of something. You may be familiar with stories such as *The Hobbit* in which the characters go on a quest to retrieve stolen treasure.

In this chapter you will explore non-fiction travel writing. This is often based on the writer's own experiences. The purpose of this type of writing varies. Some writing may provide information or attempt to persuade people to visit a place, while other writing may aim to entertain, or to share knowledge and experiences. This type of writing is often done in order to generate an income or earn a living.

Texts are also written differently to appeal to different audiences. Some of the writing is formal, while other writing is informal. Some of the writing is strictly factual, while other writing is emotive. Some travel writing is also quite literary, with writers using a range of literary devices to create a strong sense of place.

> **Spotlight on: purpose and audience**
>
> **Audience:** The people for whom the text is written; for example: young or retired, different nationalities.
>
> **Purpose:** The reason for writing the text; for example: to persuade, to share, to entertain, to earn money.
>
> The style of writing needs to suit the purpose and audience.

Activity 1.1

Work in a pair or group. Read the four texts on pages 2–4, and discuss the following questions:
- Who is the intended audience?
- What is the purpose of each text?
- Is the language formal or informal? Find examples.
- How does the language suit the purpose or intended audience?
- Do the texts provide factual information that can be checked?
- Do any of the texts attempt to persuade? In what way?

Share and discuss your ideas with others in the class.

> **HINT**
> Remember the criteria for successful group work: listen carefully, respond respectfully and take it in turns to speak.

Surfing me

Lockdown – we all know what that means now. Boredom, loneliness and not being able to move around. I think I have found a solution …

My name is Ruby. I live quite near the sea but have never really enjoyed going to the beach. Then one day my friend Mei dragged me out. 'We need to get out,' she said, 'so we are going surfing.' Surfing? Really? Me? Come on! That's just weird!

Yes me, really! We took some lessons first of course. It took me a while to even stand up on the board – on the beach, never mind on the water! It was SO tiring. But it also made me feel so free and happy. And it's healthy …

And so now I'm writing a blog about my lockdown-inspired surfing adventures. Maybe I'll also become a self-employed blog writer. (Haha!)

Watch out for my amazing photos in the next post … and a story about waves …

Reading and speaking

Poland

If you enjoy visiting fairy-tale castles and old towns with cobbled streets, then you will love Poland. If on the other hand you prefer the wild beauty of unspoiled countryside for leisure experiences, then you would also love Poland!

Poland is a huge and beautiful country in Europe that has everything – from high-tech museums and traditional architecture to medieval forests, from big cities like Warsaw and Kraków to mountain villages and beaches.

Here is a list of a few must-see places:
- The cities of Kraków, Warsaw and Gdansk
- The salt mines in Wieliczka
- The Bialowieza forest
- The Baltic beaches

For more information about flights, trains and hotels, please go to our website.

▶ The old city centre of Kraków

To celebrate its 300th birthday, Liechtenstein, Europe's least visited country and the world's sixth smallest country, has launched a 75 km walking trail which runs its entire length, through mountains, valleys and forests.

The Liechtenstein Trail: Walking the length of a country in a weekend

Our starting point was the customs office in Schaanwald – a small village sat on the Austrian border. A steep path wound its way upwards through woodland and after a few lung-busting switchbacks, the thick forest opened up to give us our first view of the Appenzell Alps – the jagged, multi-summit mountain range which was to be a constant visual companion along the trail.

Just as the path looked destined to continue rising towards the peaks, it spiralled downwards to the Rhine Valley floor, where it cut through ancient marshlands towards the municipality of Mauren. This unpredictability was to be a feature of the walk, with each day filled with tremendous variety.

After a quick coffee, the three of us continued onwards – the caffeine provided a welcome boost when the path ascended sharply. The impressive LIstory app, the official guide to the route, informed us that this stretch of the track was once a smuggling route, and with twisting, towering trees in every direction, this wasn't hard to imagine.

We eventually emerged into the tiny hilltop settlement of Hinterschellenberg, where the ruins of the appropriately named Upper Castle, built in the year 1200, made for an excellent spot to catch our breath after the climb.

Jamie Crane

1 CAPTURING THE EXPERIENCE

> **DID YOU KNOW?**
> Travel writing has been around for centuries and centuries – Pausanias (110–c.180CE) was a Greek traveller who explored the Greek empire and is known as one of the first travel writers. Another famous travel writer of old was Marco Polo, who wrote about his travels along the Silk Road from Italy to countries in the East. His work was widely read as well, but scholars question whether everything written by Marco Polo and Ibn Battuta is accurate.

In 1325CE a Moroccan scholar called Ibn Battuta set out on a hajj, or pilgrimage, to Mecca. It was a journey that at the time would have taken about 16 months. Instead, he travelled more than 117,000 km and returned home 24 years later. The book that he wrote about his travels was called *A Gift to Those Who Contemplate the Wonders of Cities and the Marvels of Travelling,* commonly known as *The Rihla* (which means 'voyage' in Arabic). It was widely read.

Extract: *The Rihla*

I set out alone, having neither fellow-traveller in whose companionship I might find cheer, nor caravan whose part I might join, but swayed by an overmastering impulse within me and a desire long-cherished in my bosom to visit these illustrious sanctuaries. So I braced my resolution to quit my dear ones, female and male, and forsook my home as birds forsake their nests. My parents being yet in the bonds of life, it weighed sorely upon me to part from them, and both they and I were afflicted with sorrow at this separation.

Ibn Battuta

Key skills

Spelling: ei or ie?

You may have learned the mnemonic 'I before e, except after c or when it sounds like "ay"'. This may help you to remember how to spell words that use e and i, but there are exceptions too, so you may have to remember some words by sight.

Activity 1.2

Work in a pair and read the following spellings. Decide which one is correct and discuss what you can do to remember this spelling. Then practise writing the words.

audience / audeince	medieval / medeival	species / speceis
caffeine / caffiene	neighbour / nieghbour	weigh / wiegh
expereince / experience	retreive / retrieve	wierd / weird
leisure / liesure	seize / sieze	

> **HINT**
> Some of the words are in the texts that you have just read, so check there if you are unsure.

Punctuation revision

Punctuation tells you how to read a text. It can show you where to pause and where to read additional information. It helps you to understand the writer's thoughts (fear, surprise, anger, joy) and intended meaning. Punctuation is used in both informal and formal writing.

Listening and writing

> **KEY WORDS**
> **exclamation mark (!)** used for emphasis; for example to indicate excitement, or shock
> **ellipsis (...)** used to emphasise a pause; for example, to indicate uncertainty
> **dash (–)** used to indicate an interruption to the main structure of a sentence
> **hyphen (-)** used to link compound words, or to show that the rest of a word is on the next line
> **parentheses/ brackets ( )** used to enclose supplemental information in a sentence

Do you remember how these punctuation marks are used? Work in a group to discuss their uses.

- exclamation mark (!)
- ellipsis (...)
- dash (–)
- hyphen (-)
- parentheses/brackets ( )

Activity 1.3

1. Work in a pair. Look at and discuss the punctuation used in 'Surfing me!' and 'The Liechtenstein Trail'.
2. Work alone to read each text aloud, paying close attention to the punctuation.
3. Read the texts aloud in a group and give each other some feedback. Who used the punctuation to good effect and how?

EXERCISE 1.1

Choose two of the texts you have read and write a short comparison, quoting examples from the text to support your comparison.

Compare:
- the purpose of each text
- the intended audiences
- the use of language and punctuation and how this is suited to the purpose.

Listening and writing

Writing a travel blog

What do you read before you travel: a travel guide or some travel blogs? A travel guide will give you detailed, accurate and practical information about a place. A travel blog may give you a better idea about whether you will enjoy visiting a place or not.

Activity 1.4

The following are titles of some recent travel blogs. Work in a pair and discuss briefly what you would expect to read about in each blog. Share your ideas with the class.

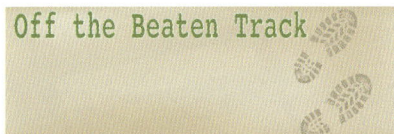

1 CAPTURING THE EXPERIENCE

Spotlight on: travel blogs

Here are some features of travel blogs:

- Are often written in the first person
- Are written about personal, unique experiences
- Are informal, chatty and conversational in style, sometimes with dialogue
- Include sensory descriptions and humour
- Include good visuals
- Play with language, sentence choice and punctuation
- Promote products which earn money for the blogger

Activity 1.5

1. Do your own research and find a travel blog that interests you. Read the features of travel blogs in the Spotlight on: box and check which of the features have been used in your chosen blog.
2. Write some notes about the features and how effectively you think they have been used.
3. Share your chosen blog and ideas with your group.

EXERCISE 1.2

1. You are going to write a travel blog about one of your own experiences. Before you do this, listen to the advice from an experienced blogger on the audio. The advice is also summarised in the graphic below.

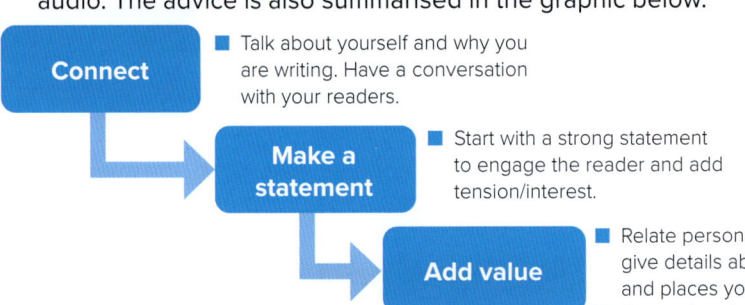

- **Connect** — Talk about yourself and why you are writing. Have a conversation with your readers.
- **Make a statement** — Start with a strong statement to engage the reader and add tension/interest.
- **Add value** — Relate personal experiences, and give details about people you met and places you visited. Remember that we live in a world of information overload!

2. Write your travel blog.
   - It should be made up of four or five paragraphs and be about 500 words long. This means that your reader can read the whole blog in a few minutes, which experts say is ideal.
   - After you have drafted the text, look at how you can manipulate the language and punctuation to show how you feel and to appeal to your readers. Add dialogue and punctuation, and vary the order of your sentences.
   - Consider the presentation and layout. If you can, include a photograph or two. This makes a big difference. If you don't have your own photo, find one online and then credit your source.
3. Post your blog on your class or school website if you have one and invite responses.

HINT
Make notes as you listen to the text, using a method of your choice. Make sure you write neatly so that you can follow your notes afterwards.

LET'S TALK
What do you know about travel blogs? Discuss these questions.
- Is the content of travel blogs accurate? How can you check this?
- How are blogs used to generate an income?
- Do you think this could affect the content of the blog?

Reading and speaking

Travel in the news

Articles about travel and interesting destinations are popular in both printed and online news media. You are going to read about a possible tourist destination and some advice about travelling to remote places.

Activity 1.6

1. Read the following article by yourself.
2. Then work in a group and discuss your responses to the text. Here are some questions to guide you:
   - Did you find this text interesting? Would you recommend it to others?
   - Does this text contain factual information? What makes you think this?
   - Do you think some people may find the text boring? If so, why?
   - What do you think is the purpose of this text?
   - Does the text make use of emotive or persuasive language? If so, why and is it successful?
   - Why do you think the writer has included quotations?
3. Share your responses with other groups.

World's longest zipline to open near Caledon

Posted by Anita Froneman on 8 September 2021

A brand new zipline, the K3, will open in the Overberg region outside Caledon in the Western Cape [in South Africa] and will bear the title of the longest zipline in the world once complete.

The thrilling ride will be 3 km in length and an estimated 500 meters from the ground at its highest point, said SA Forest Adventures who is launching the K3 in conjunction with Mossel Bay Zipline.

The project will kick off during September and is expected to be completed in time for the end of year 2021/22 summer season. 'The installation and site has been identified for a number of reasons and once phase 1 of the project has been opened and successful, the development team will start with its planning for a zipline of a record-breaking 5 km in length on the same property,' SA Forest Adventures added.

▲ Ziplining

'We are spearheading marketing the country as a premier adventure destination, with another project of international standards within our brand. We believe firmly in our country's ability to be a leader in the adventure industry, which is why we invest substantially in these projects,' said MD Clinton Lerm. 'We still firmly believe in the capacity of South Africa as a top tourism destination and a world player with other adventure destinations such as New Zealand and Canada.'

The team said the new zipline will also offer massive training and employment opportunities to the local communities.

Welcoming the launch of the K3, Western Cape Minister of Finance and Economic Opportunities, David Maynier, said: 'We are excited about the launch of the K3 which will be yet another world-class and unique tourism experience in the Western Cape, attracting both domestic and international visitors to the beautiful Overberg region.'

1 CAPTURING THE EXPERIENCE

Activity 1.7

1 What advice would you give to a friend who is embarking on a journey? Make a note of four or five points.
2 Read Dervla Murphy's advice carefully. This advice was written as a newspaper article. Compare this advice with yours. How does it differ?

Author: Dervla Murphy

Dervla Murphy (1931–2022) was an Irish travel writer who wrote many books about her experiences while travelling by bicycle or on foot through different countries throughout the world.

Extract: 'First, buy your pack animal'

In this digital age it's harder than ever to truly escape … but not impossible. Dervla Murphy, who has ventured to the ends of the earth with only the most basic provisions, explains how

The individual traveller's 'age of adventure' has long since been ended by science and technology. Now our planet's few remaining undeveloped expanses are accessible only to well-funded expeditions protected by mobile phones and helicopters – enterprises unattractive to the temperamental descendants of earlier explorers such as Mungo Park and Mary Kingsley. Happily, it's still possible for such individuals to embark on solo journeys through little-known regions where they can imagine how real explorers used to feel.

Reviewers tend to describe my most exhilarating journeys as 'adventures', though to me they are a form of escapism – a concept unfairly tainted with negative connotations. If journeys are designed as alternatives to one's everyday routine, why shouldn't they be escapist? Why not move in time as well as space, and live for a few weeks or months at the slow pace enjoyed by our ancestors? In recent decades everything has become quicker and easier: transport, communications, heating, cooking, cleaning, dressing, shopping, entertaining. However, statistics show increasing numbers of us developing ulcers, having nervous breakdowns, eating too much or too little … It's surely time to promote the therapeutic value of slow travel.

There is, of course, a certain irony here: technology has rendered the traditional simple journey somewhat artificial. Previously, those who roamed far and wide had to be isolated for long periods; now isolation is a deliberately chosen luxury. Had I died of a burst appendix in the Hindu Kush or the Simiens or the Andes, it would have been my own fault (no two-way radio) rather than a sad misfortune. Therefore, in one sense, escapist travelling has become a game – but only in one sense. The actual journey is for real: whatever happens, you can't chicken out. You're alone where you've chosen to be, and must take the consequences. (I prefer to forget that nowadays one is never quite alone. With all those satellites, the solitary traveller may be observed picking her nose in the middle of the Great Karoo.)

Dervla Murphy

Reading and writing

EXERCISE 1.3

Read the extract from the article 'First, buy your pack animal' and write your answers to the following questions.

1 Explain, using your own words, the phrases 'enterprises unattractive to the temperamental descendants of earlier explorers' and 'a concept unfairly tainted with negative connotations'.
2 According to the writer, what have been the effects of science and technology on the experience of travel?
3 Why do you think Dervla Murphy says that slow travel is 'therapeutic'?
4 Explain the 'irony' that Dervla Murphy refers to at the start of paragraph 3 (beginning 'There is, of course, a certain irony here …').
5 Write a summary of Dervla Murphy's arguments in favour of 'escapist travel' based on the extract you have read. You should use your own words and write no more than 120 words.

EXERCISE 1.4

Your cousin and three friends are planning to spend six months travelling through some far-off parts of the world before they start university. Write a letter to your cousin in which you give advice for their travels, based on Dervla Murphy's article. You should use your own words.

Reading and writing

Evoking experiences

Travel writers want to create the atmosphere of the places they visit in the minds of their readers. One way of doing this is by appealing to the readers' senses.

```
Author: Bill Bryson

Bill Bryson is an American-British author. He was born
in America but has resided in Britain for most of
his life. He made his name in travel writing when he
wrote Notes from a Small Island in 1995. He has since
published books on science, the English language and
many other non-fiction topics.
```

Spotlight on: sensory writing

Sensory writing involves describing things that you see, hear, feel, smell and taste. This adds interest and depth to descriptions as it helps readers (or listeners) to create a picture in their own minds and to 'experience' something. This can be done using simple adjectives and verbs, or by using literary devices such as similes, metaphors and onomatopoeia.

1 CAPTURING THE EXPERIENCE

EXERCISE 1.5

Read the following extract in which well-known travel writer Bill Bryson describes his impressions of the island of Capri, which is near Naples in Italy. Notice how he creates the atmosphere of the place, not just through describing what he sees, but by appealing to the reader's other senses. As you read, make notes of specific appeals to senses.

Extract: 'A traveller's impressions of Capri'

A few of the lanes were enclosed, like **catacombs**, with the upper storeys of the houses completely covering the passageways. I followed one of these lanes now as it wandered upward through the town and finally opened again to the sky in a neighbourhood where the villas began to grow larger and enjoy more spacious grounds. The path **meandered** and climbed, so much so that I grew breathless again and **propelled** myself onwards by pushing my hands against my knees, but the scenery and setting were so fabulous that I was dragged on, as if by magnets. Near the top of the hillside the path levelled out and ran through a grove of pine trees, heavy with the smell of rising sap. On one side of the path were grand villas – I couldn't imagine by what method they got the furniture there when people moved in or out – and on the other was a **giddying** view of the island: white villas strewn across the hillsides, half buried in hibiscus and bougainvillaea and a hundred other types of **shrub**.

It was nearly dusk. A couple of hundred yards further on the path rounded a bend through the trees and ended suddenly, breathtakingly, in a viewing platform hanging out over a precipice of rock – a little patio in the sky. It was a look-out built for the public, but I had the feeling that no one had been there for years, certainly no tourist. It was the sheerest stroke of luck that I had stumbled on it. I have never seen anything half as beautiful: on one side the town of Capri spilling down the hillside, on the other the twinkling lights of the **cove** at Anacapri and the houses gathered around it, and in front of me a sheer drop of – what? – 200 feet, 300 feet, to a sea of the lushest aquamarine washing against **outcrops** of jagged rock. The sea was so far below that the sound of breaking waves reached me as the faintest of whispers. A sliver of moon, brilliantly white, hung in a pale blue evening sky, a warm breeze teased my hair and everywhere there was the scent of lemon, honeysuckle and pine. Ahead of me there was nothing but open sea, calm and seductive, for 150 miles to Sicily. I would do anything to own that view, anything.

Bill Bryson

WORD ATTACK SKILLS

Work out the meaning of the following words from the context of the lines in which they appear:
- catacombs
- meandered
- propelled
- giddying
- shrub
- cove
- outcrops

Reading and writing

Activity 1.8

Discuss the following questions.
1. In what ways do the words 'wandered' and 'meandered' help you to visualise the nature of the path the writer is following?
2. Using a dictionary, check the meaning of the word 'fabulous' and then explain why you think the writer uses this word to describe the scenery around him.
3. How does the description of the viewing platform as 'a little patio in the sky' help you to share the writer's experience of the view?
4. What effect does the writer intend to achieve by placing the word 'what?' within dashes in line 48?
5. Share the notes that you made about all the different scents and smells that the writer refers to in the extract. How do these descriptions help to convey his experience?

KEY WORDS

simile a direct comparison introduced by 'like' or 'as', for example, *The smoke hung from the chimney like a drooping flag.*

metaphor an indirect comparison in which it is implied that one thing is like another, for example, *The banner of smoke flew from the factory chimney.*

onomatopoeia when the sound of a word echoes its meaning, for example, *boom*

EXERCISE 1.6
Write a short analysis of how the writer's choice of language contributes to the atmosphere, the themes and topics of the text, and the overall impact on the reader.

HINT
Writers will use a range of literary devices (**similes**, **metaphors**, **onomatopoeia**, etc.) to create an atmospheric description. When considering the effectiveness of a passage of descriptive writing it is important to consider as fully as you can how the use of these devices helps to reinforce the atmosphere the writer has created – simply identifying and listing different figures of speech is not enough.

The next extract is by the television presenter and actor Michael Palin and recounts his experiences while making a television programme about his travels through some of the wilder parts of the Himalayas. Here he describes a place called 'Tiger Leaping Gorge', a canyon on the Yangtze River in Yunnan province in south-western China.

Author: Michael Palin
Sir Michael Palin is an English actor, comedian, writer, television presenter and public speaker. He has made a number of travel documentaries and written books about his travels, which have taken him all over the world.

1 CAPTURING THE EXPERIENCE

GLOSSARY

gorge – a valley with steep, rocky walls. There is often a river running along at the bottom of the valley. The word comes from the French word *gorge*, which means throat or neck.

WORD ATTACK SKILLS

Work out the meaning of the following words from the context of the lines in which they appear:
- ethereal
- serenely
- doctored
- equine vertigo
- clamber
- trauma

Spotlight on: emotive language

Emotive language is language that is chosen in order to evoke feelings or emotions in a reader or listener. These emotions can be positive, negative or deliberately neutral. For example, using adjectives like *appalling* or *tragic* would evoke a negative response, while adjectives like *serene* or *magnificent* could evoke a positive response.

Activity 1.9

1. Before you read the following extract write down what you think you will learn from the text.
2. Write down what you already know about the Himalayas.
3. As you read, try to picture the place that is described and think about how the writer tries to evoke an experience for the reader.

Extract: 'Tiger Leaping Gorge'

This morning an **ethereal** mist lingers over the mountains, making breakfast on the terrace a chilly affair. Mr Feng De Fang produces coffee or green tea, walnuts, pancakes with smooth local honey, scrambled egg and fresh apple pie in a crisp batter.

We sit and eat too much and look out over the terraced fields below, where beans, sweetcorn and wheat defy the forces of gravity and an odd mixture of walnut and palm trees cluster around farm buildings whose stone walls are set solid and sturdy against earthquake impact.

It's a **serenely** calming view, timeless save for a mobile phone inside a **doctored** mineral-water bottle which hangs out over the balcony on the end of a stick. I ask Mr Feng if they keep it out there for security reasons but he says no, it's the only place they can get reception.

Mr Feng speaks good English, which he says he learnt from British hikers on their way through. Maybe this accounts for the fact that, as we have a group photo taken, he encourages us all with shouts of 'Lovely jubbly!' [a catchphrase from the TV series *Only Fools and Horses*].

The track continues north, clinging to the side of the rock face, the Yangtze a boiling froth 4000 feet [1220 m] below. At one point a sizeable waterfall comes bouncing off the rocks above us and we have to pick our way beneath it, over 50 yards [46 m] of wet stones. I'm most concerned about the horses but they're a lot more sure-footed than I am, perhaps there isn't such a thing as **equine vertigo**.

The stony, slippery path reaches its narrowest point. The other side of the **gorge** looms so close that perhaps a tiger might just have made it after all.

Then we're descending fast on steep and potentially lethal tracks of crumbling, chalky rock past bulky rhododendron bushes.

An almost unstoppable momentum delivers us eventually to the river as it emerges from the gorge. It's 100 yards [90 m] wide here and the jade-green stream twists and turns and eddies and swirls between banks of bleached brown boulders. We've been told that a ferry crosses here but it seems highly unlikely. There are no moorings or jetties and the water looks decidedly tricky.

Then I make out some movement on the far bank and a small, steel-hulled boat emerges from beneath the shadow of a colossal overhang and, after taking the

Reading and writing

EXERCISE 1.7

Write your answers.

1. Explain in your own words what it means to 'defy the forces of gravity'.
2. Describe and explain the effect of the figure of speech in this phrase: 'bleached brown boulders'.
3. Choose two descriptive details used by the writer that suggest the peace and calmness of the area and two that suggest the danger of the journey. Give reasons for your choices.
4. Describe in your own words how you think the writer felt about this journey. Quote words from the extract to justify your answer.

---

current in a wide arc, runs in towards us and docks by ramming its stern hard up between the rocks. Painted lettering on a metal arch at one end of the boat announces it to be the 'Tiger Leaping Gorge Ferry'. We **clamber** in and a man with a long bamboo pole and the looks and physique of a Spanish gymnast pushes us out onto the Yangtze with a flourish.

The boat seems very fragile all of a sudden. Its two outboard motors do their best but the current seems in control and swings us downstream beneath the overhang, where it's very hot and very quiet. For a moment I'm anxious. The power of the river and the power of the boat seem unfairly matched. The looming rock face above us offers no comfort.

The outboards surge, choke and surge again, but we hold our own against the current and soon we're grinding up onto a gritty beach.

An hour later we've climbed up to where the vehicles are waiting and I look back at the Yangtze, silvery in the twilight and calm and serene now after the **trauma** of the gorge, and I turn my back on it with a pang of regret.

Michael Palin

Activity 1.10

Discuss the following questions:

1. In the first paragraph of this extract, Mr Feng De Fang produces a breakfast. Describe the breakfast. Do you find anything surprising about it?
2. What do you think the writer means when he says: 'The other side of the gorge looms so close that perhaps a tiger might just have made it after all'?
3. Find some examples of emotive language used in this extract and discuss what emotional response is evoked.
4. What verb tense does the writer use in this extract? What effect do you think the use of this tense has on the impact of the writing?
5. Have you or anyone in your group had a similar experience?
   - If you have, did this help you to understand and relate to this extract? Can you explain how?
   - If you haven't had a similar experience, were you still able to picture the scene and feel what the author describes?

EXERCISE 1.8

Write a paragraph in which you try to evoke an experience of a place for other people to enjoy. Your description should be detailed and use some emotive (evocative) language. You can make use of one or two literary devices. Write in the first person and use the present tense.

EXTENSION

Work in a group.

Each member of the group re-reads one of the extracts (by Bill Bryson, page 10 and Michael Palin, pages 12–13), and uses the questions on the writing template to take short notes. Then discuss and compare the similarities and differences between the extracts.

1 CAPTURING THE EXPERIENCE

Key skills

Literary techniques

Writers and speakers use literary techniques to create an impact on readers and listeners. By now you will be familiar with literary devices such as **alliteration**, **personification**, **assonance**, onomatopoeia, similes and metaphors, and how these are used to create rhythm or sound patterns, as well as pictures in the mind of the reader.

Let's look more closely at some other literary techniques.

Euphemism

A euphemism is a device used to replace words or phrases that could make others feel uncomfortable or that could be impolite.

Euphemisms can also conceal real meanings. When Michael Palin says 'the water looks decidedly tricky', he really means that it looks very dangerous; he conceals his fear and the danger with the euphemism.

Understatement and hyperbole

Understatement is a technique that deliberately makes a situation seem less important or serious than it is. For example, describing a flood as a 'bit of rain' is an understatement. It is the opposite of hyperbole, which exaggerates a situation and makes it seem more serious or important; for example, 'I have a million things to do today.' Hyperbole is usually used to evoke strong feelings or humour and is not meant to be taken seriously or literally.

Litotes

This technique uses two negative words together; for example, 'I *don't hate* travelling.'

The writer or speaker actually means 'I enjoy travelling.'

Writers and speakers can use this technique to create humour or to understate an opinion about something so as not to appear too enthusiastic. It can also be used euphemistically so as not to seem too harsh. There is irony in saying the opposite of what you mean too.

> **KEY WORDS**
> **alliteration** the repetition of consonant sounds at the beginning of words
> **personification** giving an object or animal human characteristics
> **assonance** the use of similar sounds (particularly vowels) close together

▲ 'Under the weather' is a euphemism for being ill

Activity 1.11

Work in a pair. Discuss the techniques used, what the sentences really mean and what effect this could have on a listener or reader.
1 This bag weighs a ton!
2 That blog is not unlike mine.
3 The weather is not unpleasant at this time of the year.
4 I am not unhappy with the result.
5 She's not wrong.
6 I am so hungry I could eat a horse!
7 It could be worse.
8 The power of the river and the power of the boat seem unfairly matched.

Reading

Reading for pleasure

The author Charles Dickens is well known for his novels, but he also wrote books about his travels to America, around Britain and to Italy. These books were not travel guides but observations and opinions about what he saw and experienced, particularly the ways of life of ordinary people.

In the next extract, you will read about Dickens' first experience of a 'heavy sea' as he and his wife travelled from England to America in 1842.

Activity 1.12

1. Before you read the extract, spend a few minutes discussing the discomforts of different types of travel. What can make you uncomfortable? Why? Do you think modern travel is more comfortable than travel was in the past?
2. Do you know any other books by Charles Dickens? If so, which did you enjoy most? Which ones do you think your friends will enjoy the most? Why? What can you say about the themes he wrote about and his style of writing?

GLOSSARY
state-room – a big and luxurious room on a ship
summerset – somersault

Extract: *American Notes for General Circulation*

It is the third morning. I am awakened out of my sleep by a dismal shriek from my wife, who demands to know whether there's any danger. I **rouse** myself, and look out of bed. The water-jug is plunging and leaping like a lively dolphin; all the smaller articles are afloat, except my shoes, which are stranded on a **carpet-bag**, high and dry, like a couple of coal-barges. Suddenly I see them spring into the air, and behold the **looking-glass**, which is nailed to the wall, sticking fast upon the ceiling. At the same time the door entirely disappears, and a new one is opened in the floor. Then I begin to comprehend that the **state-room** is standing on its head.

Before it is possible to make any arrangement at all compatible with this novel state of things, the ship rights. Before one can say 'Thank Heaven!' she wrongs again. Before one can cry she IS wrong, she seems to have started forward, and to be a creature actually running of its own accord, with broken knees and failing legs, through every variety of hole and pitfall, and stumbling constantly. Before one can so much as wonder, she takes a high leap into the air. Before she has well done that, she takes a deep dive into the water. Before she has gained the surface, she throws a **summerset**. The instant she is on her legs, she rushes backward. And so she goes on staggering, heaving, wrestling, leaping, diving, jumping, pitching,

1 CAPTURING THE EXPERIENCE

WORD ATTACK SKILLS
Give modern equivalents for the following words in the text:
- ✓ rouse
- ✓ carpet-bag
- ✓ looking-glass
- ✓ expiration

throbbing, rolling, and rocking: and going through all these movements, sometimes by turns, and sometimes altogether: until one feels disposed to roar for mercy.

A steward passes. 'Steward!' 'Sir?' 'What is the matter? What do you call this?' 'Rather a heavy sea on, sir, and a **head-wind**.'

A head-wind! Imagine a human face upon the vessel's prow, with fifteen thousand **Samsons** in one bent upon driving her back, and hitting her exactly between the eyes whenever she attempts to advance an inch. Imagine the ship herself, with every pulse and artery of her huge body swollen and bursting under this maltreatment, sworn to go on or die. Imagine the wind howling, the sea roaring, the rain beating: all in furious array against her. Picture the sky both dark and wild, and the clouds, in fearful sympathy with the waves, making another ocean in the air. Add to all this, the clattering on deck and down below; the tread of hurried feet; the loud hoarse shouts of seamen; the gurgling in and out of water through the **scuppers**; with, every now and then, the striking of a heavy sea upon the planks above, with the deep, dead, heavy sound of thunder heard within a vault; – and there is the head-wind of that January morning.

I say nothing of what may be called the domestic noises of the ship: such as the breaking of glass and crockery, the tumbling down of stewards, the gambols, overhead, of loose casks … and the very remarkable and far from exhilarating sounds raised in their various state-rooms by the seventy passengers who were too ill to get up to breakfast. I say nothing of them: for although I lay listening to this concert for three or four days, I don't think I heard it for more than a quarter of a minute, at the **expiration** of which term, I lay down again, excessively sea-sick.

Not sea-sick, be it understood, in the ordinary acceptation of the term: I wish I had been: but in a form which I have never seen or heard described, though I have no doubt it is very common. I lay there, all the day long, quite coolly and contentedly; with no sense of weariness, with no desire to get up, or get better, or take the air; with no curiosity, or care, or regret, of any sort or degree, saving that I think I can remember, in this universal indifference, having a kind of lazy joy – of fiendish delight, if anything so lethargic can be dignified with the title – in the fact of my wife being too ill to talk to me … Nothing would have surprised me. If, in the

GLOSSARY
head-wind – a wind that blows in the opposite direction to the one in which you are moving
Samsons – a man famous for his great strength
scuppers – a hole in the side of a ship that allows water to drain out
Neptune – the god of water in the ancient Roman world; known as Poseidon in the Greek world

Reading

Spotlight on: choosing text references in an analysis

To justify or explain an answer, you need to refer directly to words or sentences in a text. You do not have to quote an entire sentence, but you do need to show which words you are quoting. For example:

Dickens uses personification to help the reader understand the movement of the ship, comparing it to the movement of an active person with words such as 'Before she has well done that, she takes a deep dive'.

> momentary illumination of any ray of intelligence that may have come upon me in the way of thoughts of Home, a goblin postman, with a scarlet coat and bell, had come into that little kennel before me, broad awake in broad day, and, apologising for being damp through walking in the sea, had handed me a letter directed to myself, in familiar characters, I am certain I should not have felt one atom of astonishment: I should have been perfectly satisfied. If **Neptune** himself had walked in, with a toasted shark on his trident, I should have looked upon the event as one of the very commonest everyday occurrences.
>
> Charles Dickens

EXERCISE 1.9

1. What do you think is the purpose of this text and for what audience was it written?
2. Explain as concisely as you can, using your own words, the experience Dickens describes in the first two paragraphs of this passage.
3. How do the words of the Steward in paragraph 3 create a contrast with the description in the previous paragraphs?
4. Look up the meaning of 'gambols' in a dictionary and explain why Dickens uses it to describe the sounds he hears overhead (paragraph 5).
5. Write a summary of about 80 words explaining the effects of seasickness felt by Dickens (paragraph 6).

Activity 1.13

The extract you have read is a vividly descriptive piece of writing in which the writer uses many different literary techniques such as simile, metaphor, personification, hyperbole and litotes (understatement) to create imagery and enhance his description of the voyage. He also uses humour to engage his readers.

1. Work in a group of four or five to analyse these techniques.
   Discuss which techniques you will analyse and decide who will examine each technique.
   Each person needs to find good examples from the extract that illustrate the technique and to explain the effect on the reader. Each person writes notes and a draft analysis of a technique.
2. Have a group discussion about the analyses and see what else you can add or what you can do to improve the analyses.
3. Then combine the analyses and present them for others in the class to read – either online, as a presentation or as a printed text.

LET'S TALK

Dickens and Palin use a range of literary techniques to create humour in their writing. Is humour created in the same way in modern travel blogs? If not, how is it created? What do people enjoy and find funny?

EXERCISE 1.10

Compare any two texts you have read in this chapter. Use the following headings to make your comparison:
- Purpose and audience
- Use of literary techniques
- Use of humour

EXTENSION

By bringing together information from 'A traveller's impressions of Capri' (page 10) and 'Tiger Leaping Gorge' (pages 12–13), explain as fully as you can how each extract does or does not support the ideas expressed about travel by Dervla Murphy in 'First, buy your pack animal' (page 8).

1 CAPTURING THE EXPERIENCE

Writing

Using literary techniques in travel writing

You are now going to do some more travel writing of your own.

KEY WORD
first-person narrative (using 'I') telling the story from one of the characters' point of view

Activity 1.14

Work in a group to discuss what you know about travel writing. Make notes for yourself under the headings shown below. You can use or adapt the suggestions that appear here.

Travel writing

What should I write about?
- Don't just describe the sights – explain feelings/reactions to the place
- Allow reader to share experiences

Who am I writing this for?
- Who is my audience – fellow learners/adults/people who want to share experiences? Should my writing be formal or informal?
- Will they know the place? How much detail do I need to give? What won't they know?

How should I organise my writing?
- plan – beginning, middle, end
- use **first-person narrative**, singular or plural (I/we) – maintain consistent viewpoint
- description and narrative
- interesting word choice

What literary techniques can I use to enhance my writing?
- alliteration
- similes
- litotes
- hyperbole

Writing

EXERCISE 1.11
Write an account of a visit to a place that you know well. It could be somewhere you have gone on holiday or to visit a relative or even the area in which you live. You should include:

- descriptions of your first impressions on arrival and details of the time of day when you arrived
- the place/s where you stayed and your thoughts about them
- your impressions of some of the local inhabitants
- places of interest that you visited (try to write about at least one that you enjoyed and at least one that you didn't)
- your overall opinion of the place and your thoughts and feelings when you left.

> **HINT**
> Simply describing what you did each day is most likely to make your reader lose interest!

EXERCISE 1.12
Write an account of a journey that you have made that took more than one day. You can describe a journey by any means of transport (on foot, by bicycle, road, rail, sea or aeroplane). Use a combination of narrative and **descriptive writing** and try to use literary techniques to make your descriptions vivid.

> **KEY WORD**
> **descriptive writing**
> describing a person, place, experience or thing in detail

> **HINT**
> Plan your writing. You can use a mind map to help you. Then write a draft, revise and improve your draft. Finally, write it out neatly. You may be able to word process your work, which helps to streamline the revision process.
>
> Do not focus just on what happened, but describe how the other people involved added to the experience and what your thoughts and feelings were while you were travelling.

1 CAPTURING THE EXPERIENCE

Reviewing

Reflect on your learning in this chapter.

Reading
- Which of the texts did you most enjoy reading? Why?
- Would you like to read more non-fiction travel writing?
- Write a list of the skills and techniques used by one or more of the writers in this chapter.

Speaking and listening
- How confident do you feel during the group discussions? How have your discussion skills improved since Checkpoint Stage 7?
- Do you prefer to work alone or with a partner? Does it help to listen to others and share ideas? If so, why?
- How do you adapt the way you talk and behave in different situations?

Writing
- What techniques and devices did you use in your own writing?
- Do you use a planning method before writing? How does it help?
- If you were starting your own blog, what would you write about?

Key skills
- What vocabulary have you learned?
- List five new words you have learned in this chapter and use one of them in a sentence.

Further reading and listening
If you enjoyed reading these extracts, you might enjoy:
- *Full Tilt: Ireland to India with a Bicycle* by Dervla Murphy
- searching popular travel blogs online
- *The Great Railway Bazaar* by Paul Theroux
- *Neither Here Nor There* by Bill Bryson
- *Spanish Steps* by Tim Moore
- *Travel Writing: Major Writers Travel the World* eds Linda Marsh, Michael Marland
- The Lonely Planet travel anthology
- travel-themed podcasts such as Armchair Explorer.

2 Remembering and informing

Reading
- Memoirs
- Autobiographies
- A review about the development of the Bollywood film industry
- Autobiographical poems

Speaking and listening
- Sharing personal reading preferences and interests
- Group discussion about social, cultural and historical backgrounds and contexts
- Group discussion to compare the language of two texts
- Listening to a memoir and taking notes
- Listening to, and discussing, a poem

REMEMBERING AND INFORMING

Writing
- A personal memory
- A personal memory of a trip
- Comparative analysis of two autobiographical texts
- A descriptive essay about Great Zimbabwe
- A summary of the development of the Bollywood film industry
- An informative autobiographical piece

Key skills
- Using simple, compound and compound-complex sentences
- Using participles to enhance writing
- Word choice – expanding vocabulary
- Planning, drafting, editing and finalising writing

LET'S TALK
Memoirs, autobiographies and biographies are a great way to learn more about other people's lives.
- Are you interested in other people's experiences and life stories? What makes somebody interesting to you?
- Are there any famous or well-known people that you are particularly interested in?
- Do you like to share your own experiences? Why or why not?
- Have you read any memoirs or autobiographies, or seen a film based on one?

2 REMEMBERING AND INFORMING

Speaking and reading

Remembering information

In Chapter 1 you read personal accounts of travel experiences from Charles Dickens travelling from the UK to the USA to the more recent travels of Michael Palin in China. You may also have read diaries in which people recorded their feelings and experiences of certain events while travelling.

In this chapter you will explore accounts of different life experiences in extracts from **memoirs**, **autobiographies**, poetry and other informative texts.

Memoirs and autobiographies are similar in many ways as they are based on true events, and as such they are works of non-fiction. Like travel writing, memoirs and autobiographies provide factual information as well as describing opinions and feelings. The purpose of writing may differ from travel writing and memories are not always accurate, so these texts can sometimes seem more like fiction.

> **KEY WORDS**
> **memoir** a true story or account of events, written from a personal point of view
> **autobiography** an account of a person's life, written by the person

Activity 2.1

Work in a group. Read the following short extracts aloud.
- Which of them do you think come from autobiographies or memoirs? Why do you think so? (Hint: look at the use of language.)
- What clues are there about who these people are and when and where they lived?
- Comment on the voice of the writer of each extract. What clues are there about the personality and values of each writer?
- Which do you think you might enjoy reading? Why? What would your friends enjoy?

Extract: *And Then One Day*

Today's generation, whose every sound and action is recorded from the time of their birth, and for whom the camera is part of the family, will find it hard to understand how just being photographed was such a big deal for us but it was, and for me in particular, desperate as I was to see what I really looked like.

Naseeruddin Shah (a well-known actor)

Extract: *Reaching for the Moon*

Math had always come easily to me. I loved numbers and numbers loved me, … Mine is just one tale in a long and unending chain of Black heroism and excellence that began long ago.

Katherine Johnson (NASA mathematician who helped launch Apollo 11)

Speaking and reading

Extract: Chapter 1: Mamma from *Childhood*

However vivid be one's recollection of the past, any attempt to recall the features of a beloved being shows them to one's vision as through a mist of tears – dim and blurred. Those tears are the tears of the imagination. When I try to recall Mamma as she was then, I see, true, her brown eyes, expressive always of love and kindness, the small mole on her neck below where the small hairs grow, her white embroidered collar, and the delicate, fresh hand which so often caressed me, and which I so often kissed; but her general appearance escapes me altogether.

Leo Tolstoy (a famous Russian writer)

Extract: *Memoirs: My Primary School Experience in Africa*

My first memory of that day is the sublime pleasure of playing hopscotch in the mid-morning sun with perfect strangers from Pre-Primary. I was just beginning to bond with my playmates when I was suddenly whisked away and deposited in a noisy classroom overflowing with over a hundred First Graders, proud graduates of Pre-Primary. …

Joy and laughter turned into bewilderment and sadness later that day as I came face-to-face with another group of perfect strangers: my First Grade classmates. They all knew each other from the year spent together in Pre-Primary, and I immediately became the outsider. Unlike the Pre-Primary crowd, the girls of 1R were vicious and unforgiving: kicking me in the shin and taunting me for I-knew-not-what, while I stood there wondering, 'What have I done?'

Minda Magero (a poet born in Kenya)

HINT
- Don't forget to use personal pronouns.
- Let your own voice come through in the paragraph by describing your thoughts, feelings and reactions to the event or other person carefully.
- You can use direct speech.

EXERCISE 2.1

1. Write a paragraph about an early memory of your own. For example, you could describe your memory of a specific event or describe a person who was important in your life.
2. Share your memory with your partner or group.

2 REMEMBERING AND INFORMING

Reading

Travel memoirs

Author: Laurie Lee

Laurence Edward Alan 'Laurie' Lee was an English poet, novelist and screenwriter. He is well known for his autobiographical trilogy *Cider with Rosie*, *As I Walked Out One Midsummer Morning* and *A Moment of War*.

Activity 2.2

In this extract Laurie Lee describes setting out to walk from his home in an English country village, through France to Spain in the late 1930s.

1. Before you read, comment on the title. Does it sound like a poem to you? What do you expect to read about?
2. Read the extract by yourself. As you read, note how effectively the author conveys his mixed feelings about this experience. What do you think is the purpose of this text?

WORD ATTACK SKILLS

Work out the meaning of the following words from the context of the lines in which they appear:
- gnarled
- vain-glorious
- inevitable
- squalor
- homing
- swathes

Spotlight on: understanding vocabulary

Try to read actively. If there are words that you recognise but don't fully understand, think about the following:

- Context: What is the whole sentence about?
- Grammatical form: Is it perhaps an irregular past tense form? What prefixes and suffixes have been added to the word? What do they mean?

Then check your understanding by using a dictionary or looking for the meaning in an online search. Make sure that the meaning you decide upon fits the context of the passage.

Extract: *As I Walked Out One Midsummer Morning*

The stooping figure of my mother, waist-deep in the grass and caught there like a piece of sheep's wool, was the last I saw of my country home as I left it to discover the world. She stood old and bent at the top of the bank, silently watching me go, one **gnarled** red hand raised in farewell and blessing, not questioning why I went.

At the bend of the road I looked back again and saw the gold light die behind her; then I turned the corner, passed the village school, and closed that part of my life for ever.

It was a bright Sunday morning in early June, the right time to be leaving home.

24

My three sisters and a brother had already gone before me; two other brothers had yet to make up their minds. They were still sleeping that morning, but my mother had got up early and cooked me a heavy breakfast, had stood wordlessly while I ate it, her hand on my chair, and had then helped me pack up my few belongings. There had been no fuss, no appeals, no attempts at advice or persuasion, only a long and searching look. Then, with my bags on my back, I'd gone out into the early sunshine and climbed through the long wet grass to the road.

It was 1934. I was nineteen years old, still soft at the edges, but with a confident belief in good fortune. I carried a small rolled-up tent, a violin in a blanket, a change of clothes, a tin of **treacle** biscuits, and some cheese. I was excited, **vain-glorious**, knowing I had far to go; but not, as yet, how far. As I left home that morning and walked away from the sleeping village, it never occurred to me that others had done this before me.

I was propelled, of course, by the traditional forces that had sent many generations along this road – by the small tight valley closing in around one, stifling the breath with its mossy mouth, the cottage walls narrowing like the arms of an iron maiden, the local girls whispering, 'Marry, and settle down.' Months of restless unease, leading to this **inevitable** moment had been spent wandering about the hills, mournfully whistling, and watching the high open fields stepping away eastwards under gigantic clouds …

And now I was on my journey, in a pair of thick boots and with a hazel stick in my hand. Naturally, I was going to London, which lay a hundred miles to the east; and it seemed equally obvious that I should go on foot. But first, as I'd never yet seen the sea, I thought I'd walk to the coast and find it. This would add another hundred miles to my journey, going by way of Southampton. But I had all the summer and all time to spend.

That first day alone – and now I was really alone at last – steadily declined in excitement and vigour, as I tramped through the dust towards the Wiltshire Downs a growing reluctance weighed me down. White elder-blossom and dog-roses hung in the hedges, blank as unwritten paper, and the hot empty road – there were few motor cars then – reflected Sunday's waste and indifference. High sulky summer sucked me towards it, and I offered no resistance at all. Through the solitary morning and afternoon I found myself longing for some opposition or rescue, for the sound of hurrying footsteps coming after me and family voices calling me back.

None came. I was free. I was **affronted** by freedom. The day's silence said, Go where you will. It's all yours. You asked for it. It's up to you now: You're on your own, and nobody's going to stop you. As I walked, I was taunted by echoes of home, by the tinkling sounds of the kitchen, shafts of sun from the windows falling across the familiar furniture, across the bedroom and the bed I had left.

When I judged it to be tea-time I sat on an old stone wall and opened my tin of treacle biscuits. As I ate them I could hear mother banging the kettle on the hob and my brothers rattling their tea-cups. The biscuits tasted sweetly of the honeyed **squalor** of home – still only a dozen miles away.

I might have turned back then if it hadn't been for my brothers, but I couldn't have borne the look on their faces. So I got off the wall and went on my way. The long evening shadows pointed to folded villages, **homing** cows, and after-church walkers. I tramped the edge of the road, watching my dusty feet, not stopping again for a couple of hours.

When darkness came, full of moths and beetles, I was too weary to put up the tent. So I lay myself down in the middle of a field and stared up at the brilliant stars. I was oppressed by the velvety emptiness of the world and the **swathes** of soft grass I lay on. Then the fumes of the night finally put me to sleep – my first night without a roof or bed.

I was woken soon after midnight by drizzling rain on my face, the sky black and the stars all gone. Two cows stood over me, windily sighing, and the wretchedness of that moment haunts me still. I crawled into a ditch and lay awake till dawn, soaking alone in that nameless field. But when the sun rose in the morning the feeling of desolation was over. Birds sang, and the grass steamed warmly. I got up and shook myself, ate a piece of cheese, and turned again to the south.

Laurie Lee

GLOSSARY

treacle molasses, a thick sweet liquid

affronted offended or insulted by something

2 REMEMBERING AND INFORMING

EXERCISE 2.2

1 What is this extract about? Write one sentence to explain what it describes.
2 What factual information is given in this extract?
3 Explain in your own words what the author means by these phrases:
   a 'still soft at the edges' (paragraph 3)
   b 'the cottage walls narrowing like the arms of an iron maiden' (paragraph 4).
4 Refer to the opening of the fourth paragraph and explain, in your own words, what Laurie Lee felt was the main reason for deciding to leave home.
5 By referring closely to the passage, describe and explain what Laurie Lee's feelings were during the first day of his walk.
6 In what ways did his feelings change during the second day of his walk? How does this point help you to gain a deeper understanding of his character?

EXERCISE 2.3

Read the following two sentences from the extract. Identify the types of sentences and explain what added meaning or effect the author has created in each sentence.

Then rewrite each sentence as two or three simple sentences and compare them with the originals. Is the effect the same? Why or why not?

1 'That first day alone – and now I was really alone at last – steadily declined in excitement and vigour, as I tramped through the dust towards the Wiltshire Downs a growing reluctance weighed me down.'
2 'I got up and shook myself, ate a piece of cheese, and turned again to the south.'

EXERCISE 2.4

Write a paragraph of five or six sentences about a short personal memory of a trip that you have made. Include at least one short simple sentence and one compound-complex sentence.

> **Spotlight on sentences: simple, compound and compound-complex**
>
> Do you remember?
>
> - A **simple sentence** has one verb and one clause, but it can have additional phrases.
> - A **complex sentence** has a main clause plus one or more dependent or subordinate clauses.
> - A **compound sentence** has two independent clauses of equal importance.
> - A **compound-complex sentence** has a main clause as well as dependent and independent clauses.

Activity 2.3

Laurie Lee uses different types of sentences in this extract to good effect. Sometimes the sentences echo his determination to go ahead with his plans – short simple sentences. These sentences also introduce some tension and excitement into the writing. Other sentences are long complex and compound-complex sentences with many added clauses and phrases. These echo the rambling, unsure and exploratory path he has chosen to follow by making this journey. The text becomes more philosophical as he thinks about what he is doing.

Work in a group of four. You should each read one of the sentences below and analyse it. Then share your ideas with the group.
- Identify the sentence type.
- Explain what effect the author is trying to create in the sentence.
1 'And now I was on my journey, in a pair of thick boots and with a hazel stick in my hand.'
2 'None came. I was free. I was affronted by freedom.'
3 'Naturally, I was going to London, which lay a hundred miles to the east; and it seemed equally obvious that I should go on foot.'
4 'So I got off the wall and went on my way.'

Key skills

Using participles to enhance writing

Participles are forms of verbs.
- The present participle always ends in *-ing* (*looking, seeing*).
- The past participle can take various forms, ending in *-ed, -d, -t, -en* or *-n*. Past participles often have irregular forms (*looked, seen*).
- The perfect participle uses *having* + past participle (*having looked, having seen*).

We can use present participles to make adjectives. For example:
- 'The stooping figure of my mother …'
- '… a long and searching look'

Participles are often used in (participial) phrases and clauses to add detail, to explain and integrate ideas and to add balance and depth to a sentence. They are often used as a simple way of giving a lot of information. For example:
- 'I was woken soon after midnight by drizzling rain on my face' (Instead of: by rain which was drizzling down on my face)
- 'I was excited, vain-glorious, knowing I had far to go' (Instead of: Because I knew that I had far to go)

Activity 2.4

Look at the following examples. Can you identify the participles and explain to what effect they are used?
1. 'The long evening shadows pointed to folded villages, homing cows, and after-church walkers.'
2. 'Having finished my meal, I got up and left.'
3. 'I found myself longing for … the sound of hurrying footsteps coming after me …'
4. 'I was taunted by echoes of home, by the tinkling sounds of the kitchen, shafts of sun from the windows falling across the familiar furniture.'
5. 'I tramped the edge of the road, watching my dusty feet, not stopping again for a couple of hours.'
6. 'Stopping by the side of the road, I took out my flask and drank some water.'

EXERCISE 2.5

Look at the two descriptions of memories that you have written so far in this chapter. Improve them by using participles as adjectives or in phrases and clauses that provide additional information.

> **HINT**
> Remember that the phrase always refers to the noun it precedes, for example:
> - Removing his hat, the man placed it nervously on the table.

2 REMEMBERING AND INFORMING

Listening and reading

Different times and cultures ...

Writers give factual information in memoirs and autobiographies. For example, they may give information about their activities as children. This social, cultural and historical background helps the reader to understand the experiences of the writer and how they were influenced by the situations they found themselves in. It also enriches the accounts.

Author: Nelson Mandela

Nelson Mandela (1918-2013) was a political leader in South Africa who fought against racism and apartheid. He spent 27 years in prison before serving as the president of South Africa from 1994 to 1999.

Activity 2.5

1. Before you read the extract below, discuss the meaning of the title of Mandela's autobiography. Share what you know about Mandela's life and why it was a 'long walk to freedom'.
2. Read the extract by yourself. As you read, try to imagine the childhood scenes that are described here. Think about what the purpose of this text is.
3. Complete the Word attack activity.

GLOSSARY
veld – savannah, largely unforested grassland in southern Africa

WORD ATTACK SKILLS
Work out the meaning of the following words from the context of the lines in which they appear:
- mystical
- essential
- adept
- feinting

Extract: *Long Walk to Freedom*

From an early age, I spent most of my free time in the **veld** playing and fighting with the other boys of the village. A boy who remained at home tied to his mother's apron strings was regarded as a sissy. At night, I shared my food and blanket with these same boys. I was no more than five when I became a herd-boy looking after sheep and calves in the fields. I discovered the almost **mystical** attachment that the Xhosa have for cattle, not only as a source of food and wealth, but as a blessing from God and as a source of happiness. It was in the fields that I learned how to knock birds out of the sky with a slingshot, to gather wild honey and fruits and edible roots, to drink warm, sweet milk straight from the udder of a cow, to swim in the clear, cold streams, and to catch fish with twine and sharpened bits of wire. I learned to stick-fight – **essential** knowledge to any rural African boy – and become **adept** at its various techniques, parrying blows, **feinting** in one direction and striking in another, breaking away from an opponent with quick footwork. From these days I date my love of the veld, of open spaces, the simple beauties of nature, the clean line of the horizon.

Listening and reading

LET'S TALK

Nelson Mandela talks about the attitude of his people, the Xhosa, towards cattle, as well as reminding us how important it was in this society for boys not to be seen as 'sissies' but to learn the techniques of hunting and fighting.

- How does this help the reader to understand Mandela's life?
- How is this similar to or different from your own background?
- If you wrote your memoirs or autobiography, what aspects of your social, cultural or historical background would you choose to include?

As boys, we were mostly left to our own devices. We played with toys we made ourselves. We moulded animals and birds out of clay. We made ox-drawn sledges out of tree branches. Nature was our playground. The hills above Qunu were dotted with large smooth rocks which we transformed into our own roller coaster. We sat on flat stones and slid down the face of the large rocks. We did this until our backsides were so sore we could hardly sit down. I learned to ride by sitting atop weaned calves – after being thrown to the ground several times, one got the hang of it.

Nelson Mandela

EXERCISE 2.6

1. Give three skills that Nelson Mandela learned during this period of his childhood.
2. Give three things that he particularly enjoyed about these childhood experiences and explain how these details enhance your understanding of the rest of the passage.
3. Write three short paragraphs:
   - In the first, state all the facts that you have learned about Nelson Mandela from this passage.
   - In the second, state all that Nelson Mandela tells you about his thoughts and feelings.
   - In the third, state all the facts that you have learned about the countryside in which Nelson Mandela lived as a child. Use your own words as far as possible.

Activity 2.6

Now listen to an extract written by Minda Magero which describes a young girl's experience in Kenya nearly 50 years later. Take notes as you listen for a second time.

Then think about Laurie Lee's autobiography again before you discuss and then write a comparison of all three pieces (by Laurie Lee, Nelson Mandela and Minda Magero). Consider the following:

- the differences and similarities in the viewpoints and voice in the writers' accounts of their early days
- how they describe their experiences
- their word choices and the language they use (formal/informal/literary)
- the effects they achieve through manipulation of a range of sentence types.

HINT

Think about what type of notes you should make. How should you organise them? Under headings? Your notes will help you to write a comparison.

2 REMEMBERING AND INFORMING

Key skills

Word choice

Writers choose specific words when they write. The reader needs to work out what the words mean, as the writer has used them, as well as the intended effects of using the words.

What should you, the reader, do?

- First try to find a **synonym** for the word, which should be the same part of speech.
- If you can't think of a synonym, try to explain the word in a phrase or sentence.
- Then think about the context in which the word is used. Are the words part of a literary device (such as a simile or **oxymoron**)? What is in the rest of the sentence or the sentences before or after?
- Then consider the effects of the word. What does it reveal about a writer's attitude or point of view? Does it add to the tone of the text? How do you respond to the word?

For example:

Laurie Lee talks about 'the honeyed squalor of home'. What does he mean? What effect does this achieve?

You will probably know what 'honey' is – a sweet, natural product that is good to eat. But how do you respond to the word 'squalor'? It is contradictory (an oxymoron). It implies that the home is also very dirty and neglected (and poor). So, what was the writer's view of his home? Maybe he wants to show that he had mixed feelings about it.

> **KEY WORDS**
> **synonym** a word that means the same as another word
> **oxymoron** a combination of words that seem to contradict each other
> **voice** the character and personality of the writer

Activity 2.7

Discuss the underlined words in each of the sentences below. How do you respond to the words? What effect does each word produce or help to produce?
1 'The hills above Qunu were dotted with large smooth rocks which we transformed into our own roller coaster.'
2 'Unlike the Pre-Primary crowd, the girls of 1R were vicious and unforgiving.'
3 'Joy and laughter turned into bewilderment and sadness later that day as I came face-to-face with another group of perfect strangers: my First Grade classmates.'
4 'But when the sun rose in the morning the feeling of desolation was over.'

> **EXERCISE 2.7**
> Write one or two paragraphs about an event in your early life that you remember well. Focus this time on your choice of words and what effect you want them to have on your reader.
> - Draft your description first and read it to a partner.
> - Then edit and improve the paragraph by replacing some words with more interesting words or expressions that will help to create your **voice**.

Writing and reading

Writing to inform

In autobiographies and travel writing the character and personality (voice) of the writer is important. There are other non-fiction texts in which the purpose of the passage is to convey information about a particular topic to readers in a direct and objective way. However, the voice of some writers is clear as they express opinions and feelings in their writing.

Activity 2.8

Many people have visited the ruins of Great Zimbabwe in southern Africa.

1 Work in a pair. Quickly read these short memories of three different people's experiences of the place. Discuss the opinions and facts given in each short text.

> Great Zimbabwe looks amazing in the photos but nothing beats the real thing. Layers of patterned stones towering up above as you walk. It's really huge and madly impressive.

> I remember playing hide and seek at the ruins. We climbed up the massive boulders. Of course at the time we didn't appreciate the importance of those wonderful buildings – we just had fun!

> My family visits this amazing place every year. Totally in awe of this place, inspired by the skills of the African people who built this so many hundreds of years ago. I often wonder if we could build structures like this today, even with all our modern technology. The best reason to visit Africa.

◀ The ruins of Great Zimbabwe are one of the most important archaeological sites in Africa. A great city thrived there from the eleventh century until the fifteenth century.

2 Read the following extract. As you read, think about the facts that the writer presents and look out for clues about the writer's own feelings and opinions about place.

Extract: 'The ruins of Great Zimbabwe'

The ruins of magnificent stone buildings stand at Great Zimbabwe: these ruins were once the towers and walls of a palace and the capital of a mighty and prosperous kingdom. These once-proud stone buildings were first built over 1000 years ago. Though construction continued for many hundreds of years, and the formidable walls

2 REMEMBERING AND INFORMING

reach 11 metres in height, they have been abandoned since the fifteenth century. What remains is testament to the power of human creativity, collaboration and community.

Researchers agree – the area we now call Great Zimbabwe has been inhabited for almost 2000 years. Archaeologists have discovered that early settlers farmed and mined here, sheltering in the caves, and many peoples have inhabited the area where the ruins now stand since early times.

Great Zimbabwe sits in a valley by the source of the Mutirikiwi River. The valley is fertile and the river provided water for the earliest inhabitants, as far back as the fourth century CE. The valley is rich in desirable qualities: a good and comfortable climate, fertile land, plentiful water – some estimates suggest that the settlement was once home to a settlement of over 10,000 people.

The constructions are formed not from giant boulders or great hunks of rocks. These ruins are made from countless thousands of granite chips, piled with care and great effort. Some of the stone structures are decorated by the careful arrangement of colours of black and white stones amongst the grey, showing artistry and design alongside thoughts of defence and protection. There is no evidence of roof work built in stone. Two different kinds of stonework can be seen: there are great walls that surround living enclosures, populated with huts, and then platforms made from stone fragments, to support further huts as the population increased.

It is likely the king lived amongst the ruins on the hill. Because there were no roofs, the king, the finest warriors and the priests would have lived in huts atop the hill, surrounded by these walls. This location provided excellent views and could be easily defended. Below this, in the valley beneath the hill, sits the Imba huru (Great Enclosure). This is constructed of nearly one million granite slivers, decorated in black and white, and this impressive structure remains a sight to behold.

These archaeological ruins are symbolic of Zimbabwe today. The Shona word 'dzimba' translates as 'houses' and 'mabwe' means 'stones'. As such, these formidable and beautiful ruins give Zimbabwe its name, and are a powerful symbol of the riches in these lands.

However, this is a tale of some caution. The ruins stand uninhabited. European colonists were drawn to its promises of great riches. Much has been taken, much has been damaged and lives have been lost – murder and looting all in the pursuit of gold. Great Zimbabwe's unique beauty and its archaeological significance are all that now remain.

EXERCISE 2.8

1 Using the information in the text, make notes about the:
- location and design of Great Zimbabwe
- history of the building on the site
- people who built Great Zimbabwe
- development and decline of the site.

You can do this using a method of your choice, such as a table or a mind map. Use specific and accurate vocabulary.

2 Explain the writer's opinion of Great Zimbabwe. Quote from the extract to support your explanation.

3 Do a little more research of your own about Great Zimbabwe and take notes. Then use information and vocabulary from your sources to explain what you think about Great Zimbabwe. Write about a page (300–400 words) in which you give some basic information about the place and express your own opinion as well in a subtle way.

HINT
Do not just say: 'I think that …'. Try to introduce your opinion through well-chosen adjectives or phrases.

LET'S TALK

Work in a group to compare the language of this text with the language of Laurie Lee's text on pages 24–25.
- Are the sentences constructed in the same way?
- What can you say about the word choice?
- Which text do you find more interesting to read? Why?

Reading

Reviews

Book and magazine reviews can also provide biographical and other factual information, as well as the writer's opinion.

Activity 2.9

Before you read this review in depth, skim the article quickly and answer these questions:
1 What is the review about?
2 What time frame does the review cover?
3 What biographical information might you find in the article?

WORD ATTACK SKILLS

Work out the meaning of the following words from the context of the lines in which they appear:
- advent
- blockbuster
- indigenous
- lucrative
- dubious
- exponentially
- dearth

A Brief History of Bollywood

On 7 July 1896, cinema arrived in India: this was the day when the Watkins Hotel in Bombay showed short films by the Lumière Brothers.

The first feature film was made in India in 1913. After seeing the film 'The Life of Christ' while visiting London, a printer named D.G. Phalke returned to India to make 'Raja Harishchandra', based on a story from the Mahabharata. It was a huge success and marked the real start of India's film industry.

Part of the appeal of these early films in India was that fact that, in a country of hundreds of languages, silent films had a distinct advantage in being able to reach beyond the nation's differences and provide a shared experience that would be diminished with the **advent** of sound.

The growth of the film industry was also supported by the movement of upper-class Indians between England and India in the early twentieth century. One of the first studios, Bombay Talkies, was established after the producer Himansu Rai and the actress Devika Rani returned to India. Rai's first 'talkie' film, 'Karma' (1933) starred Rani, and she went on to become India's first major female film star.

Sound arrived in Indian cinema in 'Alam Ara' in 1931. This **blockbuster** introduced song and dance as an integral part of the storytelling in the film. While sound represented a significant advance in technology, it also brought a split in the film industry in India, between the Hindi-speaking north and the Tamil and Telegu regions in the south. There are now cinemas for different dialects, such as Kanada and Gujerati. The introduction of sound also meant that Western films became less accessible in India, resulting in a drive to create an **indigenous** film industry for the cinema-hungry population.

The development of the film industry through the 1930s was similar to that of Hollywood. The studio system meant each studio employed its own directors and stars. As the industry became more **lucrative** with the arrival of sound, independent producers started tempting the most popular actors and actresses away from the studios by offering them huge amounts of cash, which sometimes came from **dubious** sources.

The golden age of Indian cinema was the 1950s: stars such as Dilip Kumar, Raj Kapoor and Dev Anand, with actresses such as Nargis, Meena Kumari, Madhubala and Vyjanthimala were in the ascendancy. The studio system produced star directors too, including Raj Kapoor, Mehbood Khan, Guru Dutt and Bimal Roy. Together they made strikingly powerful and beautiful films such as 'Devdas', 'Pyassa' and 'Kaagaz Ke Phoo', which have all stood the test of time.

The 'playback singer' emerged as a feature of the cinema in the 1940s and 1950s: the artist who did not appear on film but performed the songs to which the actors and actresses would mime. Lata Mangeshkar – known as 'the nightingale of India' – was the first playback singer who demanded that her name appeared on the film credits, and she dominated the music industry for almost 50 years. She and her sister, Asha Mangeshkar, sang almost every female part for a number of years.

▲ Lata Mangeshkar

The 1961 hit film 'Junglee' heralded the arrival of big romantic films and chocolate-box heroes such as Rajesh Khanna and Amitabh Bachchan, who ruled the screen for almost two decades. Fans went nuts for Bachchan and his fame grew **exponentially** to the point at which, when he was seriously injured in 1982, the country held its breath and, when he recovered, people lined the roads with banners stating 'God is great! Amrit lives!'.

Following the abundant years of Bollywood success, the 1980s saw a distinct drop in fortunes, with poor-quality music, a lack of star-quality in the actors who strutted their steroid-enhanced stuff and a **dearth** of good roles for actresses. Fortunately, the 1990s brought a new influx of actors, such as Aamir Khan, Shah Rukh Khan and Salman Khan, who fitted the romantic lead roles modelled by the actors of the 1960s perfectly. Strong actresses also returned to the scene, with Manisha Koirala, Madhuri Dixit and Aishwarya Rai taking on bigger roles in spectacular films.

The entertainment industry had changed significantly by this point, with cable and satellite services arriving in India providing more channels for film. Music channels screened 'filmi' music videos, increasing the influence of film music as an advertising tool.

Like every other film production centre, Bollywood must keep up with new technology and adapt to developments in entertainment, while keeping in touch with its audience. Will it continue to stand the test of time?

▲ Aishwarya Rai

Reading

EXERCISE 2.9

1. The writer of this article uses some colloquial terms. Explain the meaning of the following and then analyse the purpose and effect of the writer's choice of both formal and informal language in the passage.
   - 'went nuts over'
   - 'chocolate-box hero'
   - 'strutted their steroid-enhanced stuff'

2. Explain, using your own words, why silent films were originally better suited to the Indian market than talking ones.

3. According to the passage, what has been the main subject of Bollywood films from the 1960s onwards?

4. Although this article is intended to provide factual information, the writer's own views become apparent at times through the language used. Select at least three phrases that convey the writer's own opinions and then explain fully what the opinions are and how the choice of words reveals any suggestion of bias.

EXERCISE 2.10

Write a summary of the development of the Bollywood film industry from 1896 to the present day, using facts taken from the passage. You should write about 250 words and use your own words as far as possible.

2 REMEMBERING AND INFORMING

Speaking and listening

Remembering and giving information though poetry

Poetry can also be autobiographical, giving information about places and the poet's own life experiences. It is not always easy to tell if a poem is truly autobiographical because sometimes a poet uses pronouns such as 'I/me/we' to assume the voice of a character or a fictional identity (the persona) and reveal their feelings, inner thoughts and motivations.

```
Poet: Langston Hughes
You are already familiar with the poetry of Langston
Hughes. He was an American poet, social activist,
novelist, playwright and columnist from Missouri in
the United States of America. He became the leader of
the Harlem Renaissance which was an intellectual and
cultural revival of African American music, dance, art,
fashion, literature, theatre and politics in the 1920s
and 1930s.
```

Activity 2.10

Work in a group.
1 Read the poem 'I, Too' on page 37, which Langston Hughes wrote in 1926, and discuss these questions:
   - Do you think it is autobiographical?
   - Could 'I' and 'me' represent someone else or others?
   - What information does this poem give you about life in the USA at this time?
   - Comment on the length of the poem and the type of verse used. How does this support the message of the poem?
2 What can you say about the voice of this poet? For example, is he serious, honest, chatty, amusing or wordy? Look up and read other poems he has written.
3 Summarise what this poem is about in a sentence or two. Share and discuss your summaries with other groups.
4 Read the poem aloud in your groups. Discuss how you could do this effectively: consider verbal and non-verbal techniques.
5 What can you say about the voice of this poet? For example, is he serious, honest, chatty, amusing or wordy? Look up and read other poems he has written.

Do you remember?

The writer's voice is the style that a writer uses to convey a message or information. The writer's choice of words, length of sentences and punctuation all contribute to the voice.

'I, Too'

I, too, sing America.
I am the darker brother.
They send me to eat in the kitchen
When company comes,
But I laugh,
And eat well,
And grow strong.
Tomorrow,
I'll be at the table
When company comes.
Nobody'll dare
Say to me,
'Eat in the kitchen,'
Then.
Besides,
They'll see how beautiful I am
And be ashamed –
I, too, am America.

Langston Hughes

EXERCISE 2.11

1. Now listen to this extract from William Wordsworth's autobiographical poem 'The Prelude'.
2. Then read the poem. Don't worry about understanding every word. Focus instead on the gist of the poem.
3. What impression do you have of Wordsworth as a young child from this extract? Discuss this and quote from the poem to support your ideas.

Extract: 'The Prelude'

Fair seed-time had my soul, and I grew up	
Foster'd alike by beauty and by fear;	brought up
Much favour'd in my birthplace, and no less	
In that beloved **Vale** to which, **erelong**,	valley before long (soon)
I was **transplanted**. Well I call to mind	moved from one place to another
('Twas at an early age, **ere** I had seen	before
Nine summers) when upon the mountain slope	
The frost and breath of frosty wind had snapp'd	
The last autumnal crocus, 'twas my joy	

To wander half the night among the Cliffs
And the smooth **Hollows**, where the **woodcocks** ran | holes or empty spaces in something
brown-feathered birds

Along the open **turf**. In thought and wish | grass
That time, my shoulder all with **springes** hung, | traps for catching small animals

I was a **fell** destroyer. On the heights | mountain or hill
Scudding away from **snare** to snare, **I plied** | moving in a hurry   trap
My anxious visitation, hurrying on, | carried on my visit
Still hurrying, hurrying onward; moon and stars
Were shining o'er my head; I was alone,
And seem'd to be a trouble to the peace
That was among them. Sometimes it **befel** | happened
In these night-wanderings, that a strong desire
O'erpower'd my better **reason**, and the bird | judgement
Which was the captive of another's **toils** | efforts
Became my prey; and, when the deed was done
I heard among the solitary hills
Low breathings coming after me, and sounds
Of **undistinguishable** motion, steps | with no recognisable features
Almost as silent as the turf they trod.
Nor less in springtime when on southern banks
The shining sun had from his knot of leaves
Decoy'd the primrose flower, and when the Vales | lured
And woods were warm, was I a **plunderer** then | thief
In the high places, on the lonesome peaks
Where'er, among the mountains and the winds,
The Mother Bird had built her lodge. Though mean
My object, and **inglorious**, yet the end | shameful
Was not **ignoble**. Oh! when I have hung | inferior
Above the raven's nest, by knots of grass
And half-inch **fissures** in the slippery rock | cracks
But **ill sustain'd**, and almost, as it seem'd, | poorly kept
Suspended by the blast which blew **amain**, | full force
Shouldering the naked **crag**; Oh! at that time, | rugged rock
While on the **perilous** ridge I hung alone, | dangerous
With what strange utterance did the loud dry wind
Blow through my ears! the sky seem'd not a sky
Of earth, and with what motion mov'd the clouds!

William Wordsworth

Writing

Autobiographical writing

You are going to do some informative autobiographical writing of your own, giving accounts of things you have personally experienced.

Activity 2.11

Work in a group and discuss what you know about informative autobiographical writing. Make notes for yourselves under the following headings. You can use or adapt the suggestions that are given here.

What should I write about?
- Give the true facts of what happened and also details of how you and other people were affected by the events.
- You can write about something trivial – but recount the details clearly and honestly.
- Describe what you felt at the time when the event happened and then consider how your feelings about it have changed (or stayed the same).

What language and punctuation should I use? How can I make my own voice clear?
- Think about the tone (sad, happy, serious).
- Balance *what* you are saying with *how* you are saying it in order to engage your readers.
- Use first-person narrative, singular or plural (I/we).
- Choose vocabulary, similes, metaphors and other stylistic devices that reinforce your feelings about the experience. For example, if you found the experience upsetting, then use vocabulary to reflect your somber mood.
- Use ellipses, commas or dashes to enhance meaning, where appropriate.

How should I organise my writing?
- If you use a straightforward, chronological approach to the account, think about how and where you will make your feelings clear.
- You could start by stating what you learned from the whole experience, follow this with an account of the episode and conclude with a comment on how it has affected your subsequent outlook on life.

EXERCISE 2.12

1. Write about a time when you were involved in an accident or had an illness that prevented you from taking part in everyday activities. (It does not need to be a serious accident or illness.) You should describe how the accident or illness occurred, how you spent your time while you were recovering and what your thoughts and feelings were at the time.
2. Write about a time when you tried to help someone (either a member of your family or a friend) but your actions only made the situation worse. You should describe what the original problem was, what you hoped to do, why things went wrong and what your thoughts and feelings were.

HINT

Plan, edit and improve your writing.
- Use a mind map or notes to plan.
- Write a draft, then revise and improve your draft. Make sure you have used sentences – simple, complex or compound – to good effect.
- Finally, write the text out neatly. Make sure your handwriting is legible.
- You may be able to word process your work, which will help with the revision process. Remember to edit and proofread your work.

Reviewing

Reflect on your learning in this chapter.

Reading
- Which text did you find most engaging and why?
- You have read lots of memoirs and autobiographies in Checkpoint. Which one have you enjoyed the most?
- If you could read an autobiography about anyone, who would it be and why?
- What strategies have you learned about understanding personal accounts?

Speaking and listening
- How have your language skills developed to enable you to express your thoughts and feelings?
- What speaking and listening skills did you develop?
- Did you work successfully as part of a group? Could you improve as a group in any way? If so, how?

Writing
- Did you find it easy to express your own opinion in writing?
- Which parts of the autobiographical writing did you find enjoyable and which did you find challenging?
- If you were going to write about a personal experience, what form would you choose and why?

Key skills
- Pick five new words you have learned in this chapter that you found most interesting.
- What have you learned about a writer's choice of words? How will this inform your own writing?
- What new skills have you learned that improved your writing?

Further reading
If you enjoyed reading these extracts, you might enjoy:
- *Becoming* by Michelle Obama
- *Reaching for the Moon* by Katherine Johnson
- *Long Walk to Freedom* by Nelson Mandela
- *Unbreakable* by M.C. Mary Kom
- *Rise Up* by Stormzy
- *Cider with Rosie* by Laurie Lee

3 Writing to persuade

Reading
★ A positive perspective of a place from a website
★ A negative perspective of a place from a travel book
★ Persuasive extracts
★ A blogpost

Speaking and listening
★ Listening and discussing: what makes good persuasive writing?
★ Discussion: literary techniques used by writers
★ Debate: correct use of the term 'climate change'
★ Planning and delivering a speech

WRITING TO PERSUADE

Writing
★ A comparative description of two texts
★ Two different descriptions of one place: positive and negative
★ A reasoned argument with persuasive power

Key skills
★ Vocabulary choice: pathetic fallacy
★ Informed debate: understand the arguments
★ Grammar and sentence techniques: using gerunds
★ Choosing and following a writing process

LET'S TALK
Work in a group of three. Discuss how choosing particular words can influence readers' responses.

Below are ten words which all relate to impressions received by your nose. Which suggest to you the worst and which the most pleasant smells? In particular, think about the associations attached to the different words. Order the words on a scale of 1 to 10 from worst to most pleasant.

| aroma bouquet fragrance odour perfume smell stench stink tang whiff |

Now compare your results with other groups'. You may be surprised at the outcome.

3 WRITING TO PERSUADE

Reading

Informing and persuading

In Chapter 2 we looked at writing to convey information. Now we are going to study writing that deliberately aims to persuade readers to think in a certain way. The first two passages are both about the popular Spanish holiday resort of Benidorm.

The first extract is taken from a website that is attempting to promote Benidorm as an attractive holiday destination for potential visitors. It is, therefore, aimed at a wide audience.

> **WORD ATTACK SKILLS**
>
> Work out the meaning of the following words from the context of the lines in which they appear:
> - vibrant
> - rejuvenate
> - locale
>
> Share and compare your ideas. Research the correct definitions as a class.

> **GLOSSARY**
>
> **cosmopolitan** – a mixture of people from many different countries, suggesting sophistication
>
> **conducive** – makes something easy, or is helpful for

Extract: Visit Benidorm

Benidorm rests by the warm, clear Mediterranean Sea. It is no wonder holiday-makers smile as they reach this sunshine town. People of all ages – young children bursting with energy, parents in need of a relaxing break, or older folks just enjoying the sound of the waves – all find that Benidorm provides adventure and escape from the stresses and strains of everyday life.

Over 500,000 people enjoy the bubbly spirit of the coastal town each year, as they roam markets that are stuffed full with **vibrant** colours and goods of all kinds to interest everyone. Customers happily barter and seek to find the perfect item to take home with them, reminding them of their time in the sunshine in this tourist retreat. Whether you're looking for locally crafted trinkets or fine imports of leather items, glittering souvenirs, cheap clothing or just a prize bargain, these markets are an absolute treasure trove.

The town sits beneath the cooling shade of Puig Campana; its steep summit and forests send breezes whispering of the ancient natural retreats able to to **rejuvenate** tired minds and aching limbs. But there is a fine balance of the old and the new – bright skyscrapers punctuate the blue sky, and the beaches are all inspected to the highest modern standards of safety and cleanliness.

Like all the world's finest tourist attractions, Benidorm attracts a **cosmopolitan** mixture of people from many different countries. This is a recipe for sophistication which visitors enjoy along with the recipes for the global cuisine on offer in the many bars, cafes and restaurants all within a short stroll from the beaches bustling with energy. The carnival atmosphere lives all the summer long. Music hangs in the air, laughter rings along the streets and plazas, all **conducive** to the shared fun for all who choose to visit this **locale**.

So don't ignore the call of this Mediterranean jewel: the sun glinting off the bright waves, the gentle breezes sliding down the mountainsides and lifting the scents of the forest, and the life of the town ready to accept you into its warm embrace.

Speaking and listening

EXERCISE 3.1

Read the extract on page 42, then answer these questions.

1. Find and copy words or phrases in the passage that show the author's positive feelings towards Benidorm.
2. The passage says that Benidorm is 'a mix of the old and the new'. What do you think is the author's purpose in making this claim?
3. This sentence could be difficult to understand:

    'This is a recipe for sophistication which visitors enjoy along with the recipes for the global cuisine on offer in the many bars, cafes and restaurants all within a short stroll from the beaches bustling with energy.'

    Rewrite this sentence to make the meaning clear.
4. Write a paragraph explaining how the author uses the theme of summer to produce a positive bias. Use evidence directly from the text to support your ideas.

Speaking and listening

Using language to persuade

LET'S TALK

Work in a group of three or four. Choose one of these questions to discuss, before writing a detailed response.

- What impression does the author give of the marketplace? How does this fit with the intended outcome of the extract?
- Write a detailed analysis of the sentence that contains the phrase 'reclusive sylvan spirit'.
- The extract concludes with this phrase: 'The great attraction of Benidorm is its no-holds-barred cosmopolitan touch.' Do you think the extract convinces the reader of this idea?

HINT

Decide how to organise your discussion to achieve the goal of this task. Who should start? How will you make sure everyone is included? Will there be questions? When will these be appropriate? How will you agree the purpose of your discussion? It is worth considering all of these questions together!

EXERCISE 3.2

Listen to this extract, which is taken from *The Pillars of Hercules*. In this book, the novelist and travel writer Paul Theroux tells of his travels around the shores of the Mediterranean, giving his reactions to the places he visits. As he shares his opinions, he may also be trying to persuade his readers to agree with him.

Extract: Benidorm in winter

Benidorm was a mass of beachside high-rises, the worst place I had seen on the coast so far, worse than Torremolinos, which was slap-happy seaside tackiness of a familiar and forgivable kind. But Benidorm was ugliness on a grand scale – tall blocks of apartments, hideous hotels, winking signs, the whole place was badly built and visually unappealing. Everything that Spain was said to stand for – charm, dignity, elegance, honour, restraint – was denied in the look of Benidorm. And because this was wet chilly winter, the wide streets were empty, most of the hotels were shut, no one sat on the beach or swam in the sea: the useless horror, naked and raw in the low season, was demoralising and awful.

In 1949, Benidorm was a tiny impoverished fishing village, 'said to be an open door for smugglers', an English visitor wrote. I walked around. I had a pizza. I sat on a bench surveying the Mediterranean, and then the wind picked up and the rain began.

The rain delighted me. It whipped against the sea. It darkened the stone of the hotels and tore at the signs. It coursed down the empty streets and flooded the gutters and cut gullies through the beach sand. A bit more wind and the lights would fail, a bit more rain and it would be a real flood. And that would be the answer, the cure for Benidorm – nature's revenge, an elemental purifying storm that would wipe the place out.

It lifted my spirits to imagine the destruction of such a place, and I boarded the onward train feeling joy in my heart at the prospect of the wholesale destruction. The rain swept loudly against the side of the railway car like a shower of gravel.

From *The Pillars of Hercules* by Paul Theroux

Key skills

Vocabulary choices

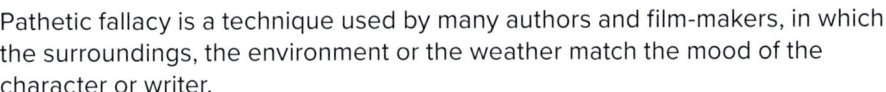

LET'S TALK

Pathetic fallacy is a technique used by many authors and film-makers, in which the surroundings, the environment or the weather match the mood of the character or writer.

Work in a group of four or five. Discuss how Paul Theroux uses pathetic fallacy in the extract about Benidorm in winter. Make some notes in response to these prompts:

- What is the purpose of the use of pathetic fallacy?
- Why do you think he says 'The rain delighted me'? What mood is he intending to convey?

Activity 3.1

1. The author appeals to the readers' senses, but which examples do you think are most effective?
   Collect a list of words or phrases and arrange them into a table like this. What do you notice?

Sight	Smell	Sound	Touch	Taste

Writing

2. Choose a sentence that uses description successfully to paint a vivid picture for you. Write a short paragraph to explain and describe how it has been successful for you.
   Share your choice with a partner. Did they pick the same as you, or did they prefer a different sentence? Listen to each other, and try to examine the sentence from their point of view.
3. Collect a list of negative words from the extract, and write a short definition of each word:

Demoralising –

Raw –

4. Paul Theroux is clearly unimpressed with Benidorm and communicates his feelings forcefully to his readers. He even says: 'It lifted my spirits to imagine the destruction of such a place.'
   Collect a list of phrases that use **hyperbole** to show the level of his feelings.
5. Find the author's description of the town's past history. How does this set the background for his current experience?

KEY WORD

hyperbole the rhetorical technique of using exaggeration for effect

> **EXTENSION**
>
> The author uses some factual descriptive sentences in a passage half-way through the extract: 'I walked around. I had a pizza. I sat on a bench …'.
>
> These do not use any negative or emotive words, yet somehow it shows his negative mood very clearly. Discuss this technique as a class. Do you think it is more or less effective than other parts of the extract?

Writing

Comparing extracts

The two passages about Benidorm are descriptive and use descriptive techniques and vocabulary to persuade readers to agree with their viewpoints.

Both writers clearly present strong views. It is unlikely that either description gives a fully accurate representation of the town but each writer is successful in presenting their intended image of Benidorm.

3 WRITING TO PERSUADE

EXERCISE 3.3

Write a comparison of the two descriptions of Benidorm and say which you find the more effective and why. In your response you should analyse:
- the details each writer gives about the town
- how the writers' language choices convey their feelings about the town and their overall impact on the reader
- the different layers of meaning within the texts, including bias, and whether or not the use of highly emotive language actually has the opposite effect to the one that is intended.

Make sure that you refer closely to both extracts in your answer to develop your analysis.

Activity 3.2

Choose one location, and write two different descriptions of the place: one positive, one negative.

Before you begin, read through the guidance below. The writing process has been split into stages with prompts to help work through the development of your writing.

Stage 1: Initial planning
Choose a location you know well, such as your hometown, or a holiday destination.
- What is the scenery like?
- What are the main buildings or locations?
- Do people work there?
- What are the main industries or activities in the area?
- Is it well known or hidden away?
- Is it quiet or busy?

Stage 2: Generate ideas and collect vocabulary
With a partner, share and describe your chosen place.

Make notes for each other on:
- sounds
- smells
- sights
- physical sensations, such as weather or the environment
- tastes.

Stage 3: Plan two versions
Work alone to write some brief notes to distinguish between the two different versions. You could use a table like the one below.
- How will you use pathetic fallacy?
- What descriptive details will you focus on?

Positive version	Negative version

Stage 4: Write a first draft
Decide on the form the writing will take:
- A guide to the area
- A travel memoir
- A diary or journal
- A tourist blog

Stage 5: Share, reflect and evaluate
Work with a partner to share your two versions.

Help each other evaluate the writing:
- Which descriptive phrases work well?
- How have they conveyed the positive and negative aspects?
- Could any parts be improved with humour, hyperbole or other techniques such as simile or metaphor?

Stage 6: Final piece
Take on board the feedback and make any corrections. Choose which format to use: best handwriting or typed and printed. Produce a final piece.

Key skills

Informed debate

The next extracts you will read are more complex and require more detailed thought.

They cover very important environmental issues, but there are some strong opinions and it can be difficult to know which argument is more accurate.

It is a vital skill to be able to understand the arguments in debates such as these, so that you can make informed decisions about key issues, rather than simply being persuaded by an author's techniques.

> **EXERCISE 3.4**
>
> When you are reading about a particular issue, there are often technical or scientific terms that need to be clearly understood.
>
> The following shows some of the terms you may read or hear in relation to environmental issues:

KEY WORD

jargon words used by a profession or group that are hard to understand

EXTENSION

Do your own research on the environment.

Ask your teacher for advice about which resources are safe and appropriate.

Scan an article or extract and collect the scientific terms and **jargon** used.

Add these to your glossary, then be prepared to share with the class.

Include an example sentence to demonstrate how each term is used correctly.

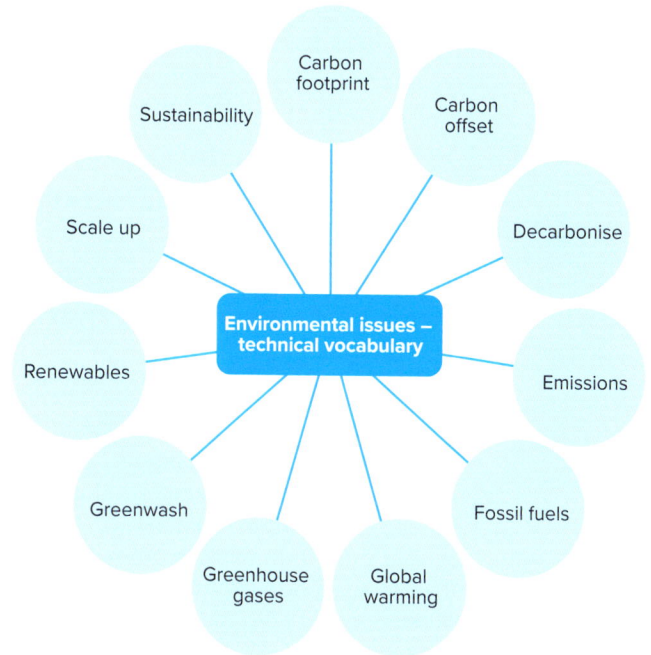

Sort these words into a table like the one below.

I know the meaning very clearly	I think I may know but I am not sure	I do not understand the term at all

Now research these terms, and write a short, factual glossary so that you can use them with accuracy and confidence.

3 WRITING TO PERSUADE

Speaking and listening

LET'S TALK

Consider these thoughts about the term 'climate change'.

> It is not strong enough. It makes it sound as if there's nothing to worry about. We should change it to 'climate emergency' or something else to show the danger.

> It is good that there is no emotion in the phrase. To be scientific, you have to ignore emotion.

> Some people think climate change is false. We need to ignore these opinions or there won't be change.

> We should listen to all arguments and opinions, but try to look for the best evidence instead of the best arguments.

In a small group, debate the use of the term 'climate change'.

How can we ensure that the topic of climate change is taken seriously?

How can we ensure that we follow the best and most accurate scientific evidence?

How will you organise future discussions to meet these goals?

EXERCISE 3.5

After your group discussion, evaluate how well you were able to follow these principles of reasoned debate:
- Was I able to make contributions?
- Did I allow others to make contributions?
- Did our group explore areas of agreement?
- Did our group explore areas of disagreement?
- How could I organise future discussions to meet these goals?

Reading

Balancing fact and emotion

The following extract is from an environmental organisation.

Activity 3.3

Work together to read the extract out loud.

You may find this is a tricky text to read aloud as there are scientific terms and mathematical statistics included. Take it in turns to read a paragraph at a time. As you read, you will have to scan ahead to be prepared for reading with accuracy.

WORD ATTACK SKILLS

Work out the meaning of the following words from the context of the lines in which they appear:
- ecological balance
- warping
- cumulatively
- agrochemicals
- toxins
- sedimentation
- mangrove forests
- exacerbating
- bottom-trawling
- coral polyp

Coral reefs

Coral reefs only occupy 0.1% of the area of the ocean but they support 25% of all marine species on the planet. The variety of life associated with coral reefs rivals that of the tropical forests of the Amazon or New Guinea.

Hundreds of millions of people rely on coral reefs for essential nutrition, livelihoods, protection from life-threatening storms and crucial economic opportunity.

About half the world's shallow water coral reefs are already gone, and without urgent action to address climate change, pollution, overfishing and destructive coastal development, these life-sustaining natural wonders could all but disappear.

What are the main threats to coral reefs?

- **Climate change:** Corals cannot survive if the water temperature is too high. Climate change has already led to sharply increased rates of coral bleaching – killing vast areas of reef – and this is predicted to increase in frequency and severity in the coming decades. Scientists estimate that at current rates of ocean warming and reef decline, most of the world's coral reefs could be lost in the next few decades.
- **Overfishing:** This affects the **ecological balance** of coral reef communities, **warping** the food chain and causing effects far beyond the directly overfished population.
- **Unsustainable coastal development:** Tourist resorts and other coastal infrastructure have been built directly on top of reefs or close enough to them to cause significant damage. The impacts of coastal development can vary widely, and **cumulatively** can put coral reef systems under considerable additional pressure. Some resorts and coastal developments empty their sewage or other wastes directly into water surrounding coral reefs.

3 WRITING TO PERSUADE

- **Pollution:** Urban and industrial waste, plastics, sewage, **agrochemicals**, and oil pollution are poisoning reefs. These **toxins** are dumped directly into the ocean or carried by river systems from sources upstream. Some pollutants increase the level of nitrogen in seawater, causing an overgrowth of algae.
- **Sedimentation:** Erosion caused by construction (both along coasts and inland), mining, logging and farming is leading to increased sediment in rivers. This ends up in the ocean, where it can 'smother' corals by depriving them of the light needed to survive. The destruction of **mangrove forests**, which normally trap large amounts of sediment, is **exacerbating** the problem.
- **Destructive fishing practices:** These include cyanide fishing, blast or dynamite fishing, **bottom-trawling**, and muro-ami (banging on the reef with sticks). Bottom-trawling is one of the greatest threats to cold-water coral reefs.

Did you know?
- The Great Barrier Reef is the largest living thing on the planet.
- Although scientists have only just begun to understand how reefs can contribute to medicine, already coral reef organisms are being used in treatments for diseases like cancer and HIV.
- The zooxanthellae algae which live symbiotically inside the **coral polyp** give the corals their amazing colours.
- Coral reefs can be found around the world and even in some places that you would not expect. In recent years scientists have discovered cold water coral reefs off the coast of Norway and deep underwater in the Mediterranean Sea.

EXERCISE 3.6
Respond to the following prompts to analyse the language choices in relation to the purpose of the text.

1. What is the main purpose of this text? What is the intended audience?
2. a   Collect three facts you have learned by reading this extract.
   b   Explain in what ways reading this has affected your emotions.
3. The text is presented a little like a glossary or a list of definitions. Explain how this relates to the intended purpose.
4. Find three different examples from the text where factual information has been presented through or alongside emotive language.
5. Which of the following opinions do you agree with?

   Write a fully justified explanation of why you agree with the opinion you have chosen. Write about 400 words.

> The emotive language is important as it highlights the urgent need for action. The author should use even more emotive language.

> The author should use less emotive language.

> The balance of emotive language and scientific facts is successful for the purpose.

Reading and writing

Complex debates on issues

The following extracts give opposing views and use a range of persuasive techniques.

Read them carefully and then answer the questions.

Extract: 'Only Nuclear Energy Can Save the Planet'

Do the maths on replacing fossil fuels: to move fast enough, the world needs to build lots of reactors

By Joshua S. Goldstein and Staffan A. Qvist

Climate scientists tell us that the world must drastically cut its fossil fuel use in the next 30 years to **stave off** a potentially catastrophic tipping point for the planet. Confronting this challenge is a moral issue, but it's also a maths problem – and a big part of the solution has to be nuclear power.

Today, more than 80% of the world's energy comes from fossil fuels, which are used to generate electricity, to heat buildings and to power car and airplane engines. Worse for the planet, the consumption of fossil fuels is growing quickly as poorer countries climb out of poverty and increase their energy use. Improving energy efficiency can reduce some of the burden, but it's not nearly enough to offset growing demand.

…

So why isn't everyone who is concerned about climate change getting behind nuclear power? Why isn't the nuclear power industry in the U.S. and the world expanding to meet the rising demand for clean electricity? The key reason is that most countries' policies are shaped not by hard facts but by long-standing and widely shared phobias about radiation.

Nuclear power is the safest form of energy by far, especially compared with coal, which continues to cause hundreds of thousands of premature deaths a year from air pollution in addition to contributing to climate change.

Over six decades, nuclear power has experienced only one fatal accident, Chernobyl in 1986 directly caused about 60 deaths and is blamed for thousands more over time from low-level radiation. That's a serious accident, but other non-nuclear industrial accidents have been worse. A hydroelectric dam failure in China in 1975 killed tens of thousands, and the 1984 Bhopal gas leak at a plant in India killed 4,000 initially and an estimated 15,000 more over time. We don't **stigmatize** those entire industries as a result.

…

> **WORD ATTACK SKILLS**
> Work out the meaning of the following words from the context of the lines in which they appear:
> - ✔ stave off
> - ✔ stigmatize
> - ✔ reactor sites
> - ✔ viable

3 WRITING TO PERSUADE

> **HINT**
> When analysing writing techniques, you should move away from the question: Do I agree with this person? Instead, think: What is the author trying to achieve, and what techniques have they used?
>
> Of course, your own opinions on issues are important, but you also need to develop the skills to read without bias.

Nor is nuclear waste the insurmountable problem that the public has been led to believe. The volumes are tiny, unlike the vast quantities of equally toxic waste from coal and other fuels. An American's entire lifetime of electricity use powered by nuclear energy would produce an amount of long-term waste that fits in a soda can. All spent fuel from U.S. reactors over the past 60 years would fit on a football field, stacked 20 feet high. Today we store spent fuel at **reactor sites** in concrete casks (radiation does not escape the concrete) that will be safe for a hundred years. After that, the waste can be burned in reactors that are currently being designed, or it can be buried permanently.

All the reasons put forward to oppose nuclear power amount to over-hyped fears that in no way stack up to the real dangers facing humanity from climate change.

Nuclear power, if scaled up in a way that has already been shown possible, would easily compete on price with fuels that pollute far more. In the coming years, the world can build reactors centrally, at factories or shipyards, using standardized designs, and achieve costs below other fuels. We can create hundreds of reactors per year world-wide and meet the world's enormous need for clean energy.

It is a win-win strategy, giving humanity its only **viable** path to stop a climate catastrophe while providing poorer countries with the energy they need to grow. It's the only strategy that adds up.

EXERCISE 3.7

1. Write a summary of this article in four or five sentences. Write a clear and accurate summary that describes the main point. Do not give your own judgement.
2. How does the passage set out to persuade you that using nuclear energy is safe?

   Collect quotations in a copy of the table below.

Purely factual evidence	Facts supported by persuasive or emotional techniques	Purely persuasive techniques

3. Make a judgement about the effectiveness of the article. Has it met its intended aim through the effective use of language? Give reasons for your evaluation.

Reading and writing

Now read the passages below and on pages 54–55 carefully and then answer the questions on page 54. These questions will help you to consider how the writers set out to persuade readers to support their views.

WORD ATTACK SKILLS

Work out the meaning of the following words from the context of the lines in which they appear:
- ✔ zeal
- ✔ dissipated
- ✔ seismically
- ✔ decommissioned

No to Nuclear Energy

Nuclear energy is expensive, dirty and dangerous.

Nuclear energy has no role to play in providing safe and clean energy for the future: the fact that it can't be seen doesn't mean that it's clean. The only way forward is renewable energy, which is better for the economy than nuclear and doesn't carry the risk of horrific accidents.

The public has become increasingly aware of the risks associated nuclear power thanks to the high-profile disasters in Chernobyl, Ukraine, in 1986 and Fukushima, Japan, in 2011. The *zeal* with which some supported nuclear energy has *dissipated* and more people than ever are aware of the fact that the risk of catastrophic meltdowns far outweighs the benefits of nuclear energy.

Compared to building renewable energy sources, such as wind or solar, the cost and time involved in building a new nuclear plant is much greater. Action is needed now to avoid the worst effects of climate change, and nuclear energy can't deliver quickly enough or cheaply enough to be the answer.

Rather than accepting the risk of disaster, we need to focus on renewables and leave the bad old days behind.

What are the dangers?

When a nuclear meltdown happens, like those in Chernobyl and Fukushima, enormous amounts of radiation are released into the surrounding environment. The levels are dangerous to human life so hundreds of thousands of people were forced to leave their homes and many may never come back. The animals living in the area may not have had even this choice to make for their survival.

Current statistics suggest that there could be a major meltdown about once every ten years.

The highly radioactive waste produced in nuclear plants is incredibly difficult to dispose of: every US waste dump leaks radiation and the nuclear plants are running out of ways to store the waste on their sites. The US has chosen a site to store its radioactive waste – Yucca Mountain in Nevada – but it is both volcanically and *seismically* active, meaning it could release radiation in the event of a quake or eruption.

The scale of building required to make nuclear energy feasible as the main source of energy is not practical: to maintain 15,000 nuclear plants, there would have to be one new plant built each day, every day, and one plant *decommissioned* each day, every day. It would also produce thousands of radioactive dead zones that could be affected by earthquakes, wastelands where uranium has been mind, and a vast amount of radioactive waste.

3 WRITING TO PERSUADE

LET'S TALK

Work in a group of three or four to complete a table like the one below.

Extract: Nuclear Energy	
Main argument	
Examples of factual information	
Examples of persuasive techniques	

EXERCISE 3.8

Write a detailed comparison of the two passages about nuclear energy (page 53 and pages 54–55). In your answer you should:
- explain clearly the intentions of each passage
- explain how the content of each passage and the tone created by the words and phrases used by each writer will influence readers (remember to quote examples)
- explore how far the writers show bias in their language and the examples they use and whether they take the views of others into consideration
- explain which passage you find more effective and why.

Reading

Blogpost

Here is another extract that describes the visit of some journalists to Chernobyl, the site that is referred to in both extracts above.

GLOSSARY
fiscal – relating to government money
power outages – failures in the power supply

WORD ATTACK SKILLS

Work out the meaning of the following words from the context of the lines in which they appear:
- ✓ mundane
- ✓ compromised
- ✓ proponents

Chernobyl: what is the truth?

The environmental campaign group Greenpeace took a group of 70 journalists from 18 countries to Chernobyl almost 25 years after the nuclear disaster in Ukraine. The experienced journalists, familiar with hard-hitting stories, were deeply disturbed by what they discovered there: often it was the **mundane** details that littered the conversations with interviewees that had the greatest impact.

For example, the Ukraine government spends somewhere between six and eight per cent of the **fiscal** budget to deal with the aftermath of the Chernobyl accident.

Each year, tens of thousands of Ukrainian children are sent to spend time in uncontaminated areas of the country for a month or more to allow their bodies to get rid of some of the caesium-137 that accumulates in their systems as a result of eating ordinary food such as berry jam, milk, mushrooms and meat.

Food sold in every market must be tested for radionuclides like caesium and strontium.

Reading

Children in the town of Rokytne, a town in western Ukraine, have **compromised** immune systems due to radionuclides, resulting in several bouts of tonsilitis each year. The deputy head doctor at the District Hospital reports that two thirds of the population in his care are affected by caesium-137 contamination in food. Rokytne is 300 km from Chernobyl – not a near neighbour.

In some areas of Ukraine, local health and sanitary stations have to make maps to show local communities where there are radiation hotspots that they should avoid.

School children are taught about radiation safety and emergency drills with gas masks.

In the face of these facts, the journalists returned home to discover that **proponents** of nuclear power were claiming that the Fukushima power plant demonstrated that nuclear energy is safe, simply because no one had (so far) been killed by radiation. This was at a time when the damage to Fukushima was not yet contained or controlled, and a huge amount of radioactive water had been dumped into the sea, with unknown consequences.

Could these people tell that to the Ukrainian doctors and parents, whose children can now only be sent for breaks to clean areas for 18 days because that is all the state can afford? Maybe they don't know that it takes 50 days for a child's body (100 days for an adult) to expel half of its radioactive caesium-137.

Could they tell it to public health officials, who are fighting hard to find money to continue monitoring food contamination?

Could they tell it to the people who would normally pick fresh blueberries in the forest, but cannot enjoy this simple pleasure due to the caesium contamination?

Do they take human life seriously? The majority of the world's current 442 nuclear power plants are getting old. Inevitably there will be leaks, errors, design flaws and **power outages**. There are no safe solutions to the problem of dealing with radioactive waste. How many more people must suffer before nuclear energy is consigned to the history books as an outdated, unnecessary and dangerous relic?

EXERCISE 3.9

1. Explain the meaning of 'radionuclide' as used in the blog. You can use a dictionary or other reference book.
2. Why do you think the author makes specific reference to the fact that the visit was made by 'experienced journalists' who were 'familiar with hard-hitting stories'?
3. Explain fully how this passage uses the powerful persuasive technique of **pathos**.

KEY WORD

pathos a rhetorical and narrative technique that aims to gain the sympathy of the audience

EXTENSION

This blogpost is written with a very clear structure, and uses repetition effectively. It could almost be the script for a speech. Work in a small group to rehearse delivering the passage as a speech, using these prompts to help you improve your performance:
- Do you need notes or a full script?
- Do you need visual aids?
- How can you adapt your voice, body language and volume to best engage the audience with the content?

3 WRITING TO PERSUADE

Key skills

Grammar and sentence techniques

Gerunds

Participles and infinitives are known as non-finite parts of the verb. However, there is one further non-finite part of the verb to consider: the gerund or verbal noun. As the name 'verbal noun' suggests, the gerund functions grammatically as a noun.

The gerund takes the same form as the present participle, so the gerund of the verb 'to sing' is 'singing'. It can be used in a sentence as either the subject or the object of another verb. For example:
- *Recycling* is an important activity.
- I enjoy *recycling*.

As it functions as a noun, a gerund can be described by an adjective. For example:
- *Frequent recycling* is a good idea.

Although the gerund functions as a noun, it still retains its character as a verb. Here is an example:
- *Recycling* paper helps to protect forests.

In this sentence, the gerund *recycling* is the subject of the verb *helps* (and is, therefore, doing the work of a noun) but also has its own object, *paper*, and so retains its verbal function.

Similarly, in the following example the gerund *scraping* has its own adverb, *noisily*, describing its action as a verb:
- *Noisily scraping* your plate can spoil other people's enjoyment of the meal.

Note that as the gerund is a noun, it must be accompanied by a possessive adjective and not by a personal pronoun.

This is a common confusion and error of expression. For example, there is a significant difference between these sentences:
- I admire his recycling. ✓
- I admire him recycling. ✗

The first sentence means that it is the person's recycling that I admire; it does not tell us that I admire the person himself. The second sentence is grammatically incorrect, but if it meant anything, it would mean that I admire the person who happens to be recycling.

EXERCISE 3.10

Practise using gerunds in your own writing, to improve the accuracy and range of your sentences.

Complete the following sentences. (You may choose to add further details to the gerunds such as adjectives or adverbs.)
- The wasting of clean water is …
- We cannot ignore the polluting of …
- If we are successful, the limiting of fossil fuel use will …
- Our saving of animals from extinction should …

Writing

A persuasive argument

EXERCISE 3.11

You are going to write your own reasoned argument with persuasive power. Use the language skills you have developed in this chapter to write a reasoned argument supported by persuasive techniques.

1 Here are some pairs of opposite opinions:

> Climate change cannot be solved until we tackle poverty.

> Climate change must be solved before we can tackle poverty.

> PE is more important to study than mathematics, because PE makes you healthy and strong.

> Mathematics is more important to study than PE, because many jobs need good academic skills.

> Teenagers should have less screen time, as it interferes with their education.

> Teenagers should have more screen time, as it helps with their education.

Choose one of these topics. Work with a partner. Discuss both opinions. Try to think of the reasons and justifications for both sides of the argument.

2 Now choose one of the opinions to support.

Follow these prompts to help you with generating ideas.

Research	Sensory information	Pathos
How will you find facts to support your argument? What sources will you be able to trust and use safely?	Remember the Benidorm extracts – sometimes the most effective writing uses specific examples that appeal to the senses.	Remember the blogpost about Chernobyl. The use of specific examples about real people can generate sympathy in the audience.

HINT

To make an effective argument, decide how to use these features to impact your audience.

EXERCISE 3.12

Choose a suitable planning process to develop your persuasive reasoned argument.

Write a first draft, then work with a partner on the improvements that are needed, before producing a final version to present to the class.

Reviewing

Reflect on your learning in this chapter.

Reading
- Would you like to visit Benidorm? What effect did the extracts about Benidorm have on you?
- Which environmental issues would you like to research further?
- Write a list of the skills and techniques you learned from these writers.

Speaking and listening
- Did you work successfully as a group? Did you feel confident to contribute? What do you think you could improve?
- What did you contribute to the debate about the term 'climate change'? Are you happy with the contribution you made? Did listening to others change your opinion?
- Did you carry out the extension activity to plan and deliver a speech? How did you find it?

Writing
- What stage of the writing process do you most enjoy (planning, drafting, improving, editing, finalising)? What do you need to work on more?
- Which did you find most satisfying to write: the negative perspective, or the positive perspective? Why?
- How do you feel about your writing skills: have they improved over the last year? Is there any aspect you would like to develop?

Key skills
- List any new techniques you have learned in this chapter. How confident do you feel about applying each one to your own work in the future?
- Which skills covered in this chapter would you like to develop further?

Further reading, listening and watching

If you enjoyed reading these extracts, you could try:
- 'I Have a Dream' Martin Luther King speech
- *No One Is Too Small to Make a Difference* by Greta Thunberg
- *The Uninhabitable Earth: Life After Warming* by David Wallace-Wells

You could try listening to these podcasts:
- *This is Working with Dan Roth* 'Bill Gates to High School Students: Solve Climate Change' (www.listennotes.com/podcasts)
- *The Mothers of Invention* 'You Probably Have Everything You Need' (www.listennotes.com/podcasts)

You could try watching these documentaries:
- *A Life on Our Planet*
- *Blue Planet*
- *A Perfect Planet*

4 Painting pictures

PAINTING PICTURES

Reading
- ★ Extracts describing places
- ★ Poems describing places
- ★ A short story describing a scary place
- ★ An informational text about a creature
- ★ Poems about creatures

Speaking and listening
- ★ Discussing descriptions in poems and songs
- ★ Discussing and comparing extracts and a poem
- ★ Discussing personal responses to writing
- ★ Listening to poems and extracts
- ★ Discussing the language in poems
- ★ Discussing writers' techniques
- ★ Reading and discussing story endings

Writing
- ★ A detailed analysis of a text
- ★ A short personal poem or a paragraph about a place
- ★ A comparison of two poems
- ★ A very short poem
- ★ A description of an encounter with a living creature

Key skills
- ★ Literary devices used in descriptive writing:
  - punctuation
  - sentence structure
  - sentence openers
  - grammar choices
  - word choices

LET'S TALK

Chapters 2 and 3 explored descriptions of places and characters in travel and autobiographical writing. In Chapter 4, you will look in more detail at how descriptions are created, in both fiction and non-fiction writing, especially descriptions of places and animals.

Work with a partner.

- ■ Think about the songs you know well. Do any of them describe places? How are the places described? What attracts you to these descriptions? Do you know the places or wish you could visit them?

- ■ Then think about a poem you have read about living creatures – animals. Is there a poem that you remember well? Why did you like it or remember it? Was it the language, the rhythm or was it perhaps a narrative?

4 PAINTING PICTURES

Speaking, listening and reading

Describing places

Activity 4.1

You will be familiar with the work of Charles Dickens (*American Notes for General Circulation*, pages 15–16) and the poet Langston Hughes (*I, Too*, page 37), and have probably also heard of the famous novel *Alice's Adventures in Wonderland* by Lewis Carroll. Discuss these authors briefly and share what you remember about their writing.

- What did they write about?
- How could you describe each writer's voice?
- What impression do you get of each writer from reading their work?
- Are they wordy? Do they use long sentences and detailed descriptions?
- Do they try to entertain their readers or are they serious?
- Would you use any of these words to describe them: honest, down to Earth, pompous?

Activity 4.2

1. Read along as you listen to the following short poem and extracts.
2. In a group of three, discuss and compare the extracts, using the questions below to guide you:
   - What is the purpose of each text?
   - What literary techniques are used and to what effect?
   - How does each writer feel about the place described?
   - What sort of language does each writer use? Is it literary or everyday? What effect does this create?
   - Does the writer use punctuation to create effects? How?
   - Does the writer use different types of sentences? To what effect?
   - Which words in the texts made the biggest impression on you?

   Now describe the voice of each writer.

'The City'

In the morning the city
Spreads its wings
Making a song
In stone that sings.

In the evening the city
Goes to bed
Hanging lights
Above its head.

Langston Hughes

Speaking, listening and reading

Extract: *Alice's Adventures in Wonderland*

The rabbit-hole went straight on like a tunnel for some way, and then dipped suddenly down, so suddenly that Alice had not a moment to think about stopping herself before she found herself falling down a very deep well.

Either the well was very deep, or she fell very slowly, for she had plenty of time as she went down to look about here, and to wonder what was going to happen next. First she tried to look down and make out what she was coming to, but it was too dark to see anything; then she looked at the sides of the well, and noticed that they were filled with cupboards and bookshelves: here and there she saw maps and pictures hung upon pegs.

Lewis Carroll

GLOSSARY
alighted – got out of a vehicle, landed
cataracts – waterfalls

Extract: *American Notes for General Circulation*

In 1842, Charles Dickens visited the USA and Canada. Here is an extract of his account of seeing the Niagara Falls for the first time and of the effect the visit had on him.

We called at the town of Erie, at eight o'clock that night, and lay there an hour. Between five and six next morning, we arrived at Buffalo, where we breakfasted; and being too near the Great Falls to wait patiently anywhere else, we set off by the train, the same morning at nine o'clock, to Niagara.

It was a miserable day; chilly and raw; a damp mist falling; and the trees in that northern region quite bare and wintry. Whenever the train halted, I listened for the roar; and was constantly straining my eyes in the direction where I knew the Falls must be, from seeing the river rolling on towards them; every moment expecting to behold the spray. Within a few minutes of our stopping, not before, I saw two great white clouds rising up slowly and majestically from the depths of the earth. That was all. At length we **alighted**: and then for the first time, I heard the mighty rush of water, and felt the ground tremble underneath my feet.

4 PAINTING PICTURES

The bank is very steep, and was slippery with rain, and half-melted ice. I hardly know how I got down, but I was soon at the bottom, and climbing, with two English officers who were crossing and had joined me, over some broken rocks, deafened by the noise, half-blinded by the spray, and wet to the skin. We were at the foot of the American Fall. I could see an immense torrent of water tearing headlong down from some great height, but had no idea of shape, or situation, or anything but vague immensity.

When we were seated in the little ferry-boat, and were crossing the swollen river immediately before both **cataracts**, I began to feel what it was: but I was in a manner stunned, and unable to comprehend the vastness of the scene. It was not until I came on Table Rock, and looked – Great Heaven, on what a fall of bright-green water! – that it came upon me in its full might and majesty.

Charles Dickens

Activity 4.3

Work in a group of four or five.
1. Each person in the group selects one of the descriptions from Activity 4.2, or another short description from a text that they enjoy.
2. Each person writes down (on a slip of paper) their personal response to the text. How did it make them feel? Did it create a clear picture in their mind? What literary techniques were used to good effect? Display the responses so that everyone in the group can read them.
3. Take turns to read your chosen descriptive text aloud. The others in the group find and match your written response to the text.
4. Discuss your views. Do others in the group agree with you? Did the way you read the extract match what you had written about it?

EXTENSION

Charles Dickens not only gives a detailed description of the majesty of Niagara Falls, but also explains the profound effect the visit had on him. Write a detailed analysis of the passage, exploring how he conveys his experience to the reader and the author's voice. You should refer closely to the passage in your answer and, in particular, consider:
- how the author's language choices contribute to his intended purpose
- the effects of the linguistic and literary techniques used
- how the use of punctuation supports the writer's intended purpose
- how the writer manipulates and adapts simple, compound, complex and compound-complex sentences for effect in his writing.

Reading, listening and writing

Using poetry to describe places

Author: W.B. Yeats

William Butler Yeats was an Irish writer. Born in 1865, he is considered one of the leading Western poets of the twentieth century. In 1923, he was awarded the Nobel Prize for Literature. His works include *The Tower* (1928) and *Words for Music Perhaps and Other Poems* (1932). Yeats died in 1939.

Activity 4.4

In the poem 'The Lake Isle of Innisfree', Yeats describes a quiet, almost magical, place in the Irish countryside that he sometimes visits.

1. Study the photograph and then read the poem by yourself. Try to get a feeling of the place that is being described. Make short notes of your first impressions.
2. Check that you understand the vocabulary. Look up words if necessary before you read the poem again, with a partner.

HINT
- Look at the structure of the poem, its rhythm and its use of rhyme.
- Look at literary devices such as onomatopoeia, assonance and alliteration. What do these help you to understand?

'The Lake Isle of Innisfree'

I will arise and go now, and go to Innisfree,
And a small cabin build there, of clay and **wattles** made;
Nine bean rows will I have there, a hive for the honey bee,
    And live alone in the bee-loud glade.

And I shall have some peace there, for peace comes dropping slow,
Dropping from the veils of the morning to where the cricket sings;
There midnight's all a glimmer, and noon a purple glow,
    And evening full of the **linnet's** wings.

I will arise and go now, for always night and day
I hear lake water lapping with low sounds by the shore;
While I stand on the roadway, or on the pavements grey,
    I hear it in the deep heart's core.

W.B. Yeats

GLOSSARY
wattles – rods or stakes interwoven with twigs for making fences, etc.
linnet – small bird of the finch family

4 PAINTING PICTURES

EXERCISE 4.1

1. Explain, using your own words, what the poet says he intends to do in the first four lines of the poem.
2. Explore fully and comment on the imagery in the phrase 'the veils of the morning'.
3. Suggest reasons why midnight might be 'all a glimmer' and noon 'a purple glow'.
4. What effect does the poet achieve by changing the usual word order in the phrase 'pavements grey'?
5. Comment on the phrase 'in the bee-loud glade'. What does it mean? How did the poet create this word? What effect does the poet achieve with it?
6. Explain as fully as you can the contrast between the last four lines and the rest of the poem. You should consider not just what the lines mean but also the language used by the poet.

Activity 4.5

1. Read the poem aloud in your group.
2. The poet sees Innisfree as a place of peace and solitude. Discuss, by referring closely to the language of the poem, how the poet creates the atmosphere of the island and its sights and sounds.

Poet: Denise Levertov

Denise Levertov (1923-97) was an award-winning British-born poet who became an American citizen. Levertov wrote and published 24 books of poetry, and also criticism and translations. She also edited several anthologies.

EXERCISE 4.2

1. Close your books and listen to this poem by Denise Levertov.
2. Write short answers to the following questions.
   a. What is the poem about?
   b. Describe the structure of the poem from what you have heard.
   c. Explain in your own words what the poet describes with these words:

> 'released autonomous
> feet pattern the streets
> in hurry and stroll; balloon heads
> drift and dive above them; the bodies
> aren't really there.'

Reading, listening and writing

'February Evening in New York'

As the stores close, a winter light
   opens air to iris blue,
     glint of frost through the smoke
     grains of mica, salt of the sidewalk.
As the buildings close, released autonomous
   feet pattern the streets
   in hurry and stroll; balloon heads
   drift and dive above them; the bodies
   aren't really there.
As the lights brighten, as the sky darkens,
   a woman with crooked heels says to another woman
   while they step along at a fair pace,
   'You know, I'm telling you, what I love best
   is life. I love life! Even if I ever get
   to be old and wheezy – or limp! You know?
   Limping along? – I'd still …' Out of hearing.
To the multiple disordered tones
   of gears changing, a dance
   to the compass points, out, four-way river.
   Prospect of sky
   wedged into avenues, left at the ends of streets,
   west sky, east sky: more life tonight! A range
   of open time at winter's outskirts.

Denise Levertov

Spotlight on: groupwork

You may have different views about this poem. That's fine. Remember:
- Take turns. Give everyone in the group a chance to speak.
- Listen carefully to what others say.
- Ask for clarification or justification.

Activity 4.6

Work in a group of three.
1. Discuss and choose a place that you all know and like (or dislike).
2. Work alone to write a short personal poem or a paragraph about the place. You could also draw a picture or add a photograph to your writing. Focus on why you like to go there. Try to create an atmosphere for your readers to help them understand why you like or dislike the place. This will help you create your own voice in the poem.
3. Share your work with the group and discuss your responses and views.

4 PAINTING PICTURES

> **HINT**
> - Look at the structure of the poem, its rhythm and its use of **enjambment**.
> - The combination of features (images, structure, word choice) helps a poet to create a scene or atmosphere.

Activity 4.7

Work in a group of four or five. Read the poem a few times and discuss these questions:

1. How are the images at the beginning of the poem different from the images at the end of the poem? What does this tell us about the place Denise Levertov describes?
2. How does the poet create the atmosphere of the city at different times?
3. Why do you think the poet uses dialogue in the poem? What effect does this have?
4. What do you think the poet feels about this city? Are the feelings perhaps ambiguous (open to more than one interpretation)? What feelings does the poem leave with you?

> **KEY WORD**
> **enjambment** – where the end of the line is not the end of the sentence, and may not require a pause

Spotlight on: planning writing

With any writing task, you need to think about what planning you need to do. Do you need to make notes? Some writing is best done spontaneously, without too much planning (a story or poem, for example), whereas other writing needs a careful plan to be successful (presenting an argument or writing a report, for example).

Before you write, ask yourself:
- Do I need to plan for this comparison?
- How best can I do this?

EXERCISE 4.3

Write a comparison of the two poems you have read, by Yeats and Levertov.

Compare the following:
- themes
- structures
- literary techniques used.

End with a personal response, saying which poem you enjoyed the most and why.

Reading and writing

Creating a sense of a place

Author: Anita Desai

Anita Desai is an award-winning English-language novelist. She was born in India in 1937 and her original name was Anita Mazumdar. She is well known for her ability to create evocative descriptions. She received a Sahitya Akademi Award in 1978 for her novel *Fire on the Mountain*.

Reading and writing

Spotlight on: short stories

A short story is a work of fiction, much shorter and more concise than a novel.

Like a novel, it has a setting, plot and characters. There are usually only a few characters and the plot is often simple, describing a single event or scene.

The plot of a short story often has a 'twist' or unexpected ending.

WORD ATTACK SKILLS

Work out the meaning of the following words using your knowledge of word families and **morphology**:
- ✔ matting
- ✔ hinges
- ✔ defunct
- ✔ unspeakable
- ✔ temerity
- ✔ muffled
- ✔ definable
- ✔ splodge
- ✔ inaction

KEY WORD

morphology the study of words and parts of words such as roots, prefixes and suffixes

GLOSSARY

Flit – an insecticide
leaves of the door – a pair of doors (a 'leaf' is a single door)

EXERCISE 4.4

The next extract is from a short story called 'Games at Twilight' by Anita Desai. In the story, some children are playing hide and seek. A timid boy named Ravi is hiding from the hunter, Raghu.

The author describes the inside of a shed in a garden in India and manages to create a sense of the scary place that Ravi has chosen as a hiding place.

Read the passage carefully and try to imagine the setting.

Extract: 'The shed'

But next to the garage was another shed with a big green door. Also locked. No one even knew who had the key to the lock. That shed wasn't opened more than once a year when Ma turned out all the old broken bits of furniture and rolls of **matting** and leaking buckets, and the white ant hills were broken and swept away and **Flit** sprayed into the spider webs and rat holes so that the whole operation was like the looting of a poor, ruined and conquered city. The green **leaves of the door** sagged. They were nearly off their rusty **hinges**. The hinges were large and made a small gap between the door and the walls – only just large enough for rats, dogs and, possibly, Ravi to slip through.

Ravi had never cared to enter such a dark and depressing mortuary of **defunct** household goods seething with such **unspeakable** and alarming animal life but, as Raghu's whistling grew angrier and sharper and his crashing and storming in the hedge wilder, Ravi suddenly slipped off the flower pot and through the crack and was gone. He chuckled aloud with astonishment at his own **temerity** so that Raghu came out of the hedge, stood silent with his hands on his hips, listening, and finally shouted 'I heard you! I'm coming! Got you –' and came charging round the garage only to find the upturned flower pot, the yellow dust, the crawling of white ants in a mud-hill against the closed shed door – nothing. Snarling, he bent to pick up a stick and went off, whacking it against the garage and shed walls as if to beat out his prey.

Ravi shook, then shivered with delight, with self-congratulation. Also with fear. It was dark, spooky in the shed. It had a **muffled** smell, as of graves. Ravi had once got locked into the linen cupboard and sat there weeping for half an hour before he was rescued. But at least that had been a familiar place, and even smelt pleasantly of starch, laundry and, reassuringly, of his mother. But the shed smelt of rats, ant hills, dust and spider webs. Also of less **definable**, less recognisable horrors. And it was dark. Except for the white-hot cracks, along the door, there was no light. The roof was very low. Although Ravi was small, he felt as if he could reach up and touch it with his fingertips. But he didn't stretch. He hunched himself into a ball so as not to bump into anything, touch or feel anything. What might there not be to touch him and feel him as he stood there, trying to see in the dark? Something cold, or slimy – like a snake. Snakes! He leapt up as Raghu whacked the wall with his stick – then, quickly realising what it was, felt almost relieved to hear Raghu, hear his stick. It made him feel protected.

4 PAINTING PICTURES

> But Raghu soon moved away. There wasn't a sound once his footsteps had gone around the garage and disappeared. Ravi stood frozen inside the shed. Then he shivered all over. Something had tickled the back of his neck. It took him a while to pick up the courage to lift his hand and explore. It was an insect – perhaps a spider – exploring him. He squashed it and wondered how many more creatures were watching him, waiting to reach out and touch him, the stranger.
>
> There was nothing now. After standing in that position – his hand still on his neck, feeling the wet **splodge** of the squashed spider gradually dry – for minutes, hours, his legs began to tremble with the effort, the **inaction**. By now he could see enough in the dark to make out the large solid shapes of old wardrobes, broken buckets and bedsteads piled on top of each other around him. He recognised an old bathtub – patches of enamel glimmered at him and at last he lowered himself onto its edge.
>
> Anita Desai

EXERCISE 4.5

Answer the following questions:

1 Explain how Ravi managed to enter the shed.
2 Work out the meaning of the following phrases as used in the second paragraph: 'a dark and depressing mortuary of defunct household goods'; 'astonishment at his own temerity'.
3 By referring closely to the third paragraph, explain Ravi's state of mind and what he found disturbing about the inside of the shed.
4 Find three examples from the passage that tell you that Ravi is a timid child. Give reasons for your choices.
5 Do you think that Ravi's feelings change in the final paragraph? Give reasons for your answer and refer closely to the passage.

Key skills

Descriptions

Writers have many tools with which they can create descriptions and a sense of place to support the purpose of their writing.

Read this passage from 'The Shed' again and look at how the author helps us to understand that Ravi is afraid, uncertain and that his thoughts are jumping around.

> Although Ravi was small, he felt as if he could reach up and touch it with his fingertips. But he didn't stretch. He hunched himself into a ball so as not to bump into anything, touch or feel anything. What might there not be to touch him and feel him as he stood there, trying to see in the dark? Something cold, or slimy – like a snake. Snakes! He leapt up as Raghu

Key skills

> whacked the wall with his stick – then, quickly realising what it was, felt almost relieved to hear Raghu, hear his stick. It made him feel protected.
>
> But Raghu soon moved away.

Look at:
- punctuation: the author uses dashes (–), commas and an exclamation mark to add information and to show the character's feelings about snakes.
- different types of sentences and questions: there is a combination of simple, compound, complex and compound-complex sentences (*What might there not be to touch him and feel him as he stood there, trying to see in the dark?*). The author uses these to vary the pace and tone of the story.
- different uses of grammar: phrases – without verbs (*Something cold, or slimy – like a snake. Snakes!*) are used to emphasise certain words and feelings.
- the sentence openers: 'Although …' and 'But …' are used to connect ideas and provide contrast.
- word choice – emotive language: 'slimy' could evoke negative or fearful feelings, 'hunched' suggests fearful, 'whacked' echoes the sudden sound of the stick.

HINT
Consider the descriptions of the inside of the shed, the things that are in it and, in particular, how the writer manipulates and adapts simple, compound, complex and compound-complex sentences to suggest the menacing atmosphere that Ravi feels and how he reacts to it.

Activity 4.8

The shed contains nothing more than old household goods and yet the writer's account of Ravi's experience turns it into a place that is scary and threatening. How does the writer achieve this effect?
1. Work in a group. Read the notes in the Key skills section above.
2. Discuss how the writer manipulates the text in the rest of the extract. Let each person in the group focus on one technique and find examples in the text.

EXERCISE 4.6
Write your own continuation and conclusion of the story. Try to continue in the same style as the original. Use punctuation in the same way and use different types of sentences to create effects (to slow down or quicken the pace, for example).

Use clues from the passage to help you imagine what might happen next.

HINT
You may want to read the endings aloud, so your audience can hear the effect of the punctuation you have used to help create atmosphere and interest.

LET'S TALK
Share your story endings with the class. Discuss which endings are the most interesting in the following ways:
- Continues in the same style
- Makes best use of sentence variety
- Uses the most evocative language
- Has the best ending (Twist? Happy? Sad? Satisfying?)

4 PAINTING PICTURES

Speaking and reading

Describing creatures

Activity 4.9

1. You will read a description of a cat from Wikipedia. Before you read, think about what information or type of description you would expect to find in this text.
2. Once you have read the extract, tell your partner about the key information you found.

> The cat (*Felis catus*) is a domestic species of small carnivorous mammal. It is the only domesticated species in the family Felidae and is often referred to as the domestic cat to distinguish it from the wild members of the family. A cat can either be a house cat, a farm cat or a feral cat; the latter ranges freely and avoids human contact. Domestic cats are valued by humans for companionship and their ability to hunt rodents. About 60 cat breeds are recognized by various cat registries.
>
> The cat is similar in anatomy to the other felid species: it has a strong flexible body, quick reflexes, sharp teeth and retractable claws adapted to killing small prey. Its night vision and sense of smell are well developed. Cat communication includes vocalizations like meowing, purring, trilling, hissing, growling and grunting as well as cat-specific body language.

3. Now look at the description of a cat in the poem 'Cat-rap' by Grace Nichols. What sort of description do you think you will get in this poem? Share your ideas and then read the poem.

Poet: Grace Nichols

Grace Nichols was born in Guyana, in South America, and later emigrated to the United Kingdom. Her award-winning collections of poetry are popular with adults and children. Her poetry is influenced by Guyanese and Amerindian folklore and the Caribbean culture in which she grew up.

Speaking and reading

> **DID YOU KNOW?**
> Macavity the Mystery Cat, also called the Hidden Paw, is a fictional character created by the poet T.S. Eliot in his book *Old Possum's Book of Practical Cats*. Macavity breaks laws and has a wild side to him. Macavity also appears in the musical *Cats*, which is based on T.S. Eliot's book.

'Cat-rap'

Lying on the sofa
all curled and meek
but in my furry-fuzzy head
there's a rapping beat.
Gonna rap while I'm napping
and looking sweet
gonna rap while I'm padding
on the balls of my feet

Gonna rap on my head
gonna rap on my tail
gonna rap on my
you know where.
So wave your paws in the air
like you just don't care
with nine lives to spare
gimme five right here.

Well, they say that we cats
are killed by curiosity,
but does the moggie mind?
No, I've got suavity.
When I get to heaven
gonna rap with Macavity,
gonna find his hidden paw
and clear up that mystery.

Nap it up
scratch it up
the knack is free
fur it up
purr it up
yes that's me.

The meanest cat-rapper you'll ever see.
Number one of the street-sound galaxy.

Grace Nichols

Activity 4.10

Work alone or in a pair and give a performance of 'Cat-rap'. You can choose to learn the poem or to read it aloud. In your performance use body language and facial expressions to help your audience understand the cat as described in the poem.

> **HINT**
> The rhythm in this poem is the key to a good performance. Experiment with how you read or recite the poem until it sounds like a rap poem.
> - Vary the flow and pace. What works best: rapping quickly or slowly?
> - Identify the rhyme scheme and rhyming words. Do you need to emphasise the rhyming words as you rap?
> - Find your voice. Who is the narrator and what would he/she sound like?
> - How will you use gestures and body movement? Can you be catlike as you recite?
>
> Try to bring out the contrast between the 'curled and meek' cat on the sofa at the beginning and the wilder image of the cat who wants to be a rapper.

4 PAINTING PICTURES

Author: D.H. Lawrence

David Herbert Lawrence (1885-1930) was an English writer and poet. Many of his novels are based in Nottinghamshire, where he grew up, although he travelled the world in his later life and is also an acclaimed travel writer.

In the following poem, the poet describes an event that happened to him while living on the Mediterranean island of Sicily. Through carefully chosen words and images, he vividly recreates his encounter with a snake, as well as using the experience to analyse his own response.

Listen to and read the poem and then answer the questions that follow.

GLOSSARY
fissure – a crack or narrow opening in a rock or stone
Etna – the active volcano on the island of Sicily
perversity – a strange feeling of wanting to behave in an unacceptable way
paltry – small, mean
'And I thought of the albatross' – a reference to the poem *The Rime of the Ancient Mariner* by Samuel Taylor Coleridge, which describes the horrifying events that result when a sailor for no reason kills an albatross – a bird considered by sailors to bring good luck.
expiate – to make amends for something you have done wrong

'Snake'

A snake came to my water-trough
On a hot, hot day, and I in pyjamas for the heat,
To drink there.

In the deep, strange-scented shade of the great dark carob-tree
I came down the steps with my pitcher
And must wait, must stand and wait, for there he was at the trough before me.

He reached down from a **fissure** in the earth-wall in the gloom
And trailed his yellow-brown slackness soft-bellied down, over the edge of the stone trough
And rested his throat upon the stone bottom,
And where the water had dripped from the tap, in a small clearness,
He sipped with his straight mouth,
Softly drank through his straight gums, into his slack long body,
Silently.

Someone was before me at my water-trough,
And I, like a second comer, waiting.

He lifted his head from his drinking, as cattle do,
And looked at me vaguely, as drinking cattle do,
And flickered his two-forked tongue from his lips, and mused a moment,
And stooped and drank a little more,
Being earth-brown, earth-golden from the burning bowels of the earth
On the day of Sicilian July, with **Etna** smoking.

The voice of my education said to me
He must be killed,
For in Sicily the black, black snakes are innocent, the gold are venomous.

And voices in me said, If you were a man
You would take a stick and break him now, and finish him off.

But must I confess how I liked him,
How glad I was he had come like a guest in quiet, to drink at my water-trough
And depart peaceful, pacified, and thankless,
Into the burning bowels of this earth.

Was it cowardice, that I dared not kill him? Was it **perversity**, that I longed to talk to him?
Was it humility, to feel so honoured?
I felt so honoured.

And yet those voices:
If you were not afraid, you would kill him!

And truly I was afraid, I was most afraid, But even so, honoured still more
That he should seek my hospitality
From out the dark door of the secret earth.

He drank enough
And lifted his head, dreamily, as one who has drunken,
And flickered his tongue like a forked night on the air, so black,
Seeming to lick his lips,
And looked around like a god, unseeing, into the air,
And slowly turned his head,
And slowly, very slowly, as if thrice adream,
Proceeded to draw his slow length curving round
And climb again the broken bank of my wall-face.

And as he put his head into that dreadful hole,
And as he slowly drew up, snake-easing his shoulders, and entered farther,
A sort of horror, a sort of protest against his withdrawing into that horrid black hole,
Deliberately going into the blackness, and slowly drawing himself after,
Overcame me now his back was turned.

I looked round, I put down my pitcher,
I picked up a clumsy log
And threw it at the water-trough with a clatter.
I think it did not hit him,
But suddenly that part of him that was left behind convulsed in undignified haste.
Writhed like lightning, and was gone
Into the black hole, the earth-lipped fissure in the wall-front,
At which, in the intense still noon, I stared with fascination.

4 PAINTING PICTURES

> And immediately I regretted it.
>
> I thought how **paltry**, how vulgar, what a mean act!
> I despised myself and the voices of my accursed human education.
>
> **And I thought of the albatross**
>
> And I wished he would come back, my snake.
>
> For he seemed to me again like a king,
> Like a king in exile, uncrowned in the underworld,
> Now due to be crowned again.
>
> And so, I missed my chance with one of the lords
> Of life.
> And I have something to **expiate**:
> A pettiness.
>
> D.H. Lawrence

EXERCISE 4.7

1. What are the poet's first reactions when he sees the snake at his water-trough? Quote from the poem to support your answer.
2. In the early stages of the poem, do you think the poet is in any danger from the snake? Quote from the poem (especially from stanzas 3 and 5) in your answer.
3. What do you understand by the poet's reference to the 'voice of my education' and 'voices in me'? Explain how he reacts to these voices.
4. Why do the voices say that the poet should kill the snake and what are the poet's reasons for not wanting to?
5. Explain how the poet's language reflects the contrast between the behaviour of the snake and the attitudes suggested by the voices.
6. What reason does the poet give for throwing the log at the snake?
7. Comment on the phrase 'I picked up a clumsy log'. In what ways can a log be said to be 'clumsy'?
8. How does the rhythm of the stanza beginning 'I think it did not hit him' reflect the actions described? Look at the enjambment and the length of the sentences, for example.
9. Describe the poet's thoughts and feelings at the end of the poem, after the snake has gone. Comment particularly on what you understand by the last two lines.

> **HINT**
> Explore the effects created by the use of alliteration, assonance and onomatopoeia, and the rhythm of the two sections of the poem.

EXERCISE 4.8

1. Look closely at the description of the snake in stanza 3. How does the poet use language to create a picture in your mind?
2. Consider closely the language used by the poet to describe the snake and his thoughts about it in the first part of the poem, as far as the line 'And climb again the broken bank of my wall-face' (stanza 12) and compare it with the language of the remaining stanzas.

Writing and speaking

Descriptions in poetry and prose

> **EXERCISE 4.9**
> Write a description of an encounter with a living creature. You can write a poem or prose of any length but the description should make use of literary techniques. You should also use different types of sentences to help create your description.

Activity 4.11

1 Work in a group to brainstorm some ideas about how you could describe the photograph below. Focus on four key ideas and then find words to describe these.

2 Look at this example:

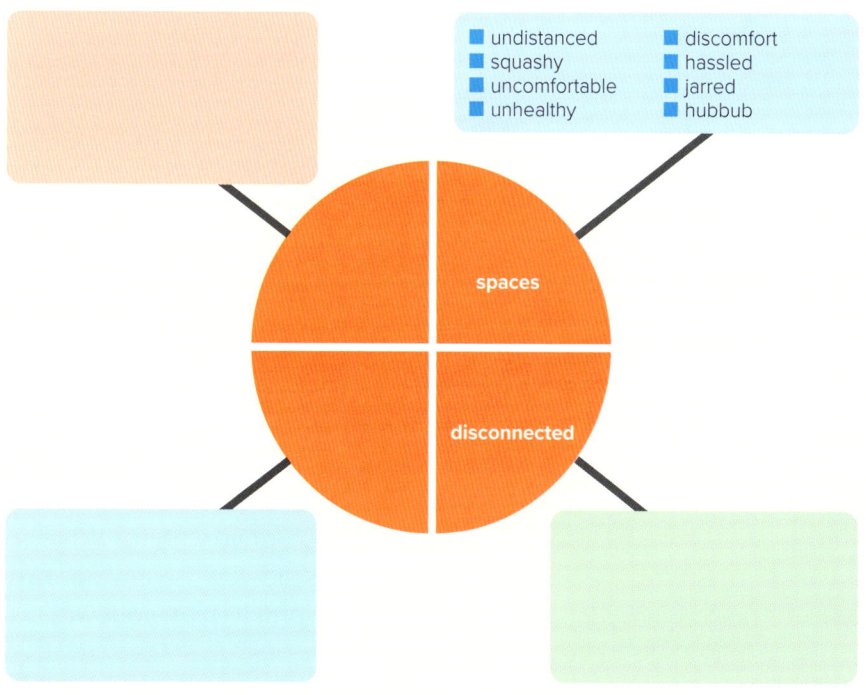

- undistanced
- squashy
- uncomfortable
- unhealthy
- discomfort
- hassled
- jarred
- hubbub

> **HINT**
> You can decide whether you should write spontaneously or whether you need to draw up a plan when writing your description.

> **KEY WORD**
> **haiku** a short poem with three lines and 17 syllables; lines 1 and 3 have five syllables each and line 2 has seven syllables.

3 Find other words that you could use with the words you have written, to create literary effects like assonance, metaphor and alliteration; for example:
- socially squashed
- distinctly disconnected
- crowded commuter can.

4 Discuss all the words you have written down. Choose the best words and make up a very short poem (a **haiku**, for example) or write two or three sentences to describe the photo using literary techniques to enhance the description.

> **HINT**
> Do not try to use all the words you have written down in your poem or sentences.

4 PAINTING PICTURES

Activity 4.12

You are going to read or recite your prose or poetic descriptions.
1. Discuss this with your group and decide what will work best; for example:
   - Should you perform as a group or individually?
   - Could one person perform the work while others act or add music to the performance?
2. After your performance, invite feedback from your audience.
   - What worked well for them and helped them understand the descriptions?
   - What did not work so well?

Reviewing

Reflect on your learning in this chapter.

Reading
- Which of the texts did you prefer?
- Would you read any of the texts again, or choose to read more from that author or poet?
- Write a list of the descriptive writing skills and techniques you learned from one or more of these authors.

Speaking and listening
- Performing a rap may have been a new experience for you. How did you feel about it? What did you have to consider? Did you use non-verbal techniques?
- Do you find it helpful to share ideas in a small group or with a partner? Why?
- Which speaking and listening skills would you like to develop?

Writing
- Do you enjoy descriptive writing? Why?
- What techniques did you use in your own writing?
- Do you find it helpful to plan your writing first, or do you prefer to be spontaneous?

Key skills
- What vocabulary have you learned? List five new words you have learned.
- This chapter covered these literary devices used in descriptive writing:
  - punctuation
  - sentence structure
  - sentence openers
  - grammar word choice.
- Do you have a clear understanding of each, or is there an area in which you would like to do more practice?

5 Advertising

Reading
★ Advertisements
★ 'Why advertisers target children'
★ 'Euphemisms'
★ Extract: 'Politics and the English Language' by George Orwell

Speaking and listening
★ A discussion about advertising
★ Performing a radio advert
★ Listening to, and evaluating, other groups' radio adverts
★ A class discussion reviewing previous opinions about advertising

Writing
★ A comparative analysis of two adverts
★ A rhetorical devices glossary
★ A single-page brochure
★ A one-minute radio or podcast advert

Key skills
★ Vocabulary development: jargon, rhetorical devices
★ Research: types of adverts and literary devices
★ Creating adverts

LET'S TALK
As a class, discuss these statements. Do you agree or disagree? How do you feel about adverts?

> I am not influenced by adverts. I just buy what I need and decide for myself.

> Adverts are so annoying. When they pop up on my phone, I just ignore them.

> I really enjoy some adverts. They make buying stuff seem exciting.

> My brother works in advertising. He makes a lot of money. It's big business.

5 ADVERTISING

Speaking and listening

Why advertise?

Activity 5.1

1. Jot down your first thoughts about advertising.
   - What adverts can you remember?
   - What adverts do you like or not like?
   - How do you feel when you see an advert?
   - Do you have any questions about advertising?
   - What is the purpose of advertising?
2. Share your answers with a partner.
   - Do you have any shared opinions?
   - Are there any famous adverts you both know?
   - What products do you notice being advertised most regularly?
   - Where do you see adverts?
   - Do you think adverts affect you? Do they influence what you buy or want to buy?
3. Now work in a group of five or six, with the following roles:

◀ Note-recorder – This person should keep notes on the group's ideas, then feed back to the group at the end of the discussion.

◀ Chairperson – This person should make sure that everyone is involved in the discussion, and that the discussion stays focused.

◀ Contributors – Take turns to share your opinions and ask questions.

◀ Summariser – This person will present the group's overall findings to the whole class at the end.

As a group, think about the following questions:
- What are the main sources of advertising?
- What is the purpose or the purposes of advertising?
- How much are you affected by advertising?
- What are the features that make an effective advert?
- Overall, is your opinion of advertising positive, negative or neutral? What reasons and justifications can you give.

4. Each group takes a turn to feed back to the class. Carefully listen to each person.
   - Does anything that you have heard change your opinions?
   - Is there agreement or disagreement? About what?
   - Are there any strong feelings in the class?
5. Use your notes, and the outcomes of the class discussion, to write a short personal reflection with the title:
Thoughts after listening to the class discussion on advertising

Key skills

Vocabulary development

When thinking about advertisements it is important to keep some key words in mind.

The following list contains some jargon from the world of advertising:

GLOSSARY OF ADVERTISING JARGON

target audience – Specific adverts are aimed at certain groups of people who are called the target audience. For example, toy adverts may be aimed at children, and this will affect the style and form of the advert.

branding – The name of a product or business may become famous, fashionable or trusted. The better the branding, the more recognisable the name or product. The brand may include the name, logo and also the associated lifestyle. There are many famous brands for fast foods, clothing and perfume.

prime time – The time periods in a day or week when most people watch media. This may include big occasions, such as sports events. Companies pay more to advertise their products during prime-time events, as they reach a bigger audience.

USP – USP stands for unique selling point. If a product has a USP, then the advertisers can use this to convince people that they should have the product.

advertising agency – An advertising agency is a company that specialises in creating and distributing adverts for a range of different businesses or products.

slogan – A slogan is a word or phrase that is easy to remember and is chosen to draw your attention to the product being advertised. (The word 'slogan' comes from an Old Irish word meaning 'battle cry'.)

jingle – Advertising jingles are catchy tunes and phrases that become associated with a particular product.

lifestyle – A product may be associated with a certain lifestyle, so that people may believe that buying the product will help them live a certain kind of daily life.

endorsements – Using film stars or sporting personalities to claim that they use the product being advertised is called celebrity endorsement. The idea is that their fans will then buy the product in order to be like the person, or because they trust the person is telling the truth.

Some advertisers use members of the public to endorse the product, so that the target audience may think 'They are just like me, so I will like this too.'

product placement – A film or television show may include branded products in the background or as props. Examples of this include cars driven by action heroes, watches or phones used by characters and soft drinks that appear on the screen.

influencers – Celebrities or internet vloggers, who use social media, use or present products and talk about them positively to 'influence' others.

5 ADVERTISING

> **EXERCISE 5.1**
>
> Write a detailed response to each question.
>
> 1 What famous **brands** do you know? Make a list and share your ideas with a partner. For each brand, suggest the **lifestyle** with which the brand is associated.
> 2 What do you think is more effective: celebrity **endorsement** or endorsement by a member of the public? Give reasons for your answer.
> 3 Do you think **product placement** is effective? How do you think it could persuade people to buy a certain product?
> 4 Would you be interested in becoming an **influencer**? If so, what area would you like to work in? If not, what would put you off doing so?

Reading and writing

Comparing adverts

Here is a simple advertisement for a car.

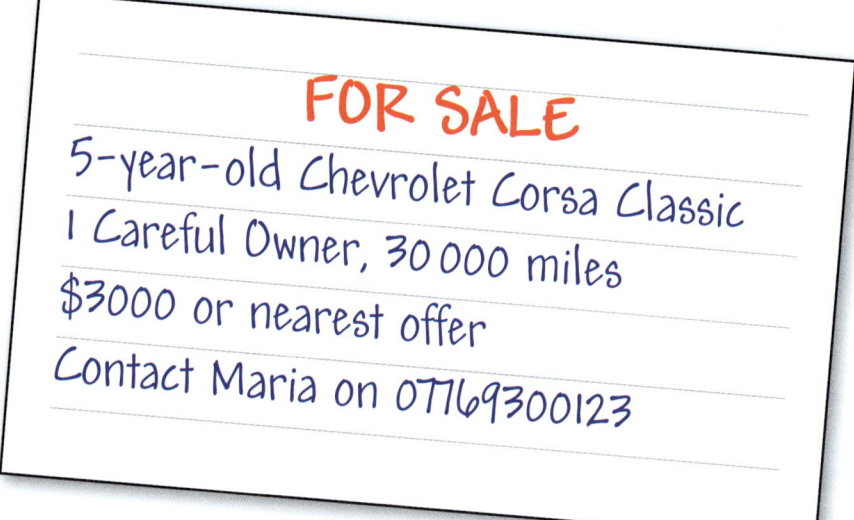

You would probably see an advert like this either in a shop window or in the classified advertisements section of a local newspaper, where it would be placed among many similar advertisements all aimed at members of the public who might be considering buying a used car – the **target audience**. This type of advertisement is intended simply to draw attention to its subject (the used car for sale) and to provide some very straightforward information about it: how much the car is on sale for and the person to contact if you are interested in buying it. It makes no serious attempt to persuade you to buy the car (although the reference to one *careful* owner could be intended to do so).

Reading and writing

EXERCISE 5.2
Now carefully read this advertisement for a new car and answer the questions that follow.

EXERCISE 5.3
Now that you have answered the questions in Exercise 5.2, think about how this advertisement differs from the one for the Chevrolet Corsa on page 80.

Write a detailed comparison and analysis of the adverts, using some of the phrases from the glossary:
- USP
- lifestyle
- branding
- slogan
- target audience.

HINT
Choose how to plan and structure your writing to make the comparisons clear.

1 This is a fictional magazine advertisement. In what country do you think the advertisement would be published? Give your reasons.
2 Who do you think is the target audience for this advertisement?
3 What effect is achieved by the statement above the picture?
4 What do you understand by the phrase 'national stereotypes'? Explain fully how the text of the advertisement uses national stereotypes to engage its readers. In particular, think about the tone of the language in the advertisement.
5 In what other way does the advertisement try to interest people in the Daschler Grun?
6 What information does the advertisement give you about the car itself? Do you find this particularly helpful?
7 Explain fully what you think is added to the advertisement by the photo and the graph below it.
8 Explain what you think the purpose of the advertisement is. How successful do you think it is in achieving this purpose?

5 ADVERTISING

> **KEY WORDS**
> **rhetoric** the process of using the resources of language to persuade an audience to agree with a particular point of view
> **oratory** the art of skilful and effective public speaking. A good orator is likely to make use of rhetoric

Speaking

Rhetorical techniques used in advertising

Rhetoric has a long history and the ancient Greeks and Romans in particular wrote detailed books about how it should be used in practice. Listed below are some of the main devices that they considered necessary for a successful **orator** to use (there are many more that have not been listed!).

GLOSSARY OF RHETORICAL DEVICES

rhetorical question (erotema) – A rhetorical question is asked in order to make a point, not to get an answer; for example: *How can you resist such a fabulous offer?*

emotive language – Words and phrases can be used to cause an emotional response, persuading an audience to invest in an idea or product; for example: *All is not lost, there's still a chance that you could be a lucky winner.*

parallel structures – A parallel structure uses the same pattern of words to present two or more ideas. This can be used to emphasise a comparison or contrast; for example: *Give a man a fish and you feed him for a day; teach a man to fish and you feed him for a lifetime.*

sound patterns – These techniques can be used to make something memorable or to put something, such as a brand or a product, in the forefront of the audience's mind. There are various different types, such as:
- alliteration – a series of two or more words beginning with the same consonant; for example: *Bigger, better ... buy it now!*
- assonance – a series of words that repeat the same vowel sound; for example: *Dine at night by candlelight.*

contrast – Contrast can be used to emphasise the differences between two people, places or things; for example: *Sometimes we have to be cruel to be kind.*

description and imagery – These devices can be used to evoke an emotion such as a desire; for example, using metaphor, simile or personification: *Let the warm arms of the sunshine caress you while you lie back and enjoy the never-ending view of white sand and blue sea.*

rule of three (tricolon) – This technique can be used to make something memorable or put something, such as a brand or a product, in the forefront of the audience's mind. It uses a pattern of three phrases in parallel; for example: *to live, to love, to be.*

repetition (anaphora) – Repetition can also be used to make something memorable or put something, such as a brand or a product, in the forefront of the audience's mind; for example: *Easy come, easy go.*

hyperbole – Hyperbole is used to exaggerate for effect, and is a useful persuasive device; for example: *A feeling so good, it'll last a lifetime.*

anecdote – An anecdote is a brief narrative describing an interesting or amusing event. Storytelling can engage an audience or make the audience feel that they can relate to the experience, for example: *Three rugby matches a week, and caked head to toe in mud every time, I didn't think I'd ever get the dirt out of this kit, then I discovered ...*

Key skills

> **EXTENSION**
> 1 Look again at the adverts that you used in Activity 5.2 and search for examples of rhetorical devices.
> 2 Collect examples from the texts and create your own glossary of rhetorical terms, to refer to and use in your own writing.

Activity 5.2

Bring a newspaper or magazine advertisement to the lesson, and work in a small group.
1 Explain to the other members of your group what it is that you find particularly effective about the advertisement you have chosen.
2 As a group, discuss whether the advertisement achieves its effect more through providing information or through its entertainment value.
3 When each group has discussed all of their advertisements, work together as a class to put them into categories according to the type of product they are advertising.
4 Consider the different categories of items that are advertised. Are more expensive, luxurious objects or more mundane items (such as toothpaste or washing powder) advertised more heavily? Why might this be?

Key skills

Research

Activity 5.3

In a small group, find examples of the different types of advertisements listed in the table below.

Copy and complete the table by examining and discussing what techniques are used for each one and how effective they are.

Type	Description	Techniques used	Comments (e.g. effectiveness)
Magazine			
Newspaper			
Television			
Radio			
Billboard			
Public information			
Internet			

5 ADVERTISING

> **HINT**
> Adverts have a clear target audience, but this can lead to some damaging stereotypes. Look carefully at your chosen advert. Does it use stereotypes or prejudice or discrimination; for example, are women shown doing household chores or men driving fast sports cars?
>
> If this is the case, you should include your thoughts about this in your written response.

> **EXTENSION**
> Choose one or two of the advertisements from your list. You are going to write a detailed analysis of how they set out to persuade their audience to buy the product(s) that are being advertised.
>
> You can decide the best way to plan your analysis, but do consider the following points:
> - What particular social group or groups is the advertisement aimed at and what assumptions, if any, does it make about them? For example, is the advertisement appealing to people's wish to be rich or fashionable?
> - What is actually being advertised? What specific feature of the product does the advertisement focus on and why?
> - Where and when was the advertisement published and how does this relate to its target audience?
> - What sentence types are used: simple, compound, complex …? What other grammatical decisions have been made by the author of the adverts?
> - How is language used in the advertisement and what is its effect? Does the advertisement contain hyperbole – words such as 'miracle', 'sensational', 'magic'? Does it use more aggressive words or phrases such as 'challenge' or 'buy now before it's too late'? Remember, advertisements frequently use a direct tone of address; the second-person pronoun 'you' features prominently in many advertisements.
> - What images does the advertisement use and why?
> - Do you personally find the advertisements persuasive? Why?

Reading

Children and advertising

This extract explains ways in which advertisers target children of all ages. Read it carefully and then answer the questions that follow.

Why advertisers target children

Research shows that children see around 10,000 television adverts each year. While advertisers often claim that their advertisements are intended for parents to see, rather than their children, they still commit huge amounts of money to tell children about their latest snack, toy or game.

Why do advertisers do this? It's not as if children have a lot of money to spend:

pocket money isn't generally that generous. But most advertisers are in it for the long game: they know that, one day, those kids will be adults with their own disposable incomes, who might then recommend the same brands to their children.

And advertising to children doesn't just reach pocket money. Advertisers are wise to the strength of 'pester power', which means that even small children can persuade their harassed parents to buy something different if they are targeted with successful marketing techniques.

Psychologists have discovered that children as young as two years old are able to ask their parents for particular products – even specific brands – while they are out shopping. The products that young children are most likely to request are breakfast cereals, drinks and toys – which happen to be the type of items that advertisers tend to promote with child-friendly ad campaigns.

Reaching children at an early age can allow advertisers to create brand loyalty – and sometimes that loyalty lasts a lifetime, so it is invaluable for those brands. Amazingly, children are able to recognise different brand logos from the age of three, and may express a preference for one brand over another from two years old.

Unsurprisingly, parents are increasingly worried about the amount of advertising seen by children each day: social scientists believe that most children can identify more than 400 company brand names by the age of ten.

Studies show that the vast majority of parents think too much advertising is aimed at children, particularly as there are more ways for advertisers to reach them than ever before. In addition to the many TV channels specifically for children (but also often watched by parents), there is online advertising, advertising on social media platforms and branded books and comics.

Children are now growing up in the most **media-saturated** period of human history. They may begin watching television before they begin walking and talking, and play with toys that feature characters from TV shows within their first year of life. Toddlers may play with a parent's smartphone or even have their own tablet computer.

The **proliferation** of modern media means advertisers now have ever more ways to change children into consumers. Clever targeting of children through animated adverts or interactive online games mean that children who spend a lot of time watching TV or on the internet are more likely to want toys that appear in adverts than those who don't consume so much media.

The way in which children respond to adverts depends on their age and **sophistication**. In their early years, children don't understand money or buying power, so they don't realise that adverts are designed to persuade them to buy a product. Advertisers are skilled at making adverts that blend into the world of children, such as using cartoon animals that make an advert look similar to an actual TV programme. To a child, the advert and the TV programme may be **indistinguishable**.

Studies show that children under the age of eight have no way to **critically evaluate** claims that are made in adverts. By presenting products in an emotive way – such as showing breakfast cereal in an exciting, animated setting – advertisers suggest appealing ideas about the products to children. However,

---

WORD ATTACK SKILLS

Work out the meaning of the following words and phrases from the context of the lines in which they appear:
- ✔ media-saturated
- ✔ proliferation
- ✔ sophistication
- ✔ indistinguishable
- ✔ critically evaluate
- ✔ peer group
- ✔ implicit
- ✔ cachet

5 ADVERTISING

children don't realise that the actual product may not really be so exciting.

When children grow older and start interacting in **peer groups**, the advertisers tend to change their approach to show products as 'must-have' items. They might show a group of happy kids using their product – with the **implicit** message that if a child doesn't have the product, they won't be accepted or liked by their peers. Psychologists have found that this can cause tension within families and within peer groups as parents may feel guilty if they do not buy the product, and children may feel inadequate or excluded from a peer group if they do not have a product that others already have.

As children become teenagers, their understanding of how advertising works becomes more sophisticated and they can be much more critical of adverts. This can make them really difficult to advertise to. Rather than simply wanting to be accepted by their peers, teens are starting to create their own identity and align themselves with whatever peer group is the most 'cool' to them. Consequently, advertisers have to create a **cachet** of cool, without trying too hard – which is even less appealing than not being cool enough.

Some advertisers address this problem by making adverts that don't actually look like adverts: they might create an advert in a magazine or on a sticker that directs teens to a website that isn't easy to find or isn't immediately identifiable as advertising, where the teens can find out more. Making the advertising less obvious allows teens to feel that they have found out something that other people don't know about – they know more than their peers or parents do. This taps into teens' tendency to rebel, to market expensive products to them.

Reading

EXERCISE 5.4

1. Write a summary of paragraphs 1–7 explaining why advertisers target children and how children and their parents respond to such advertising. Use your own words as far as possible and write about 150 words.

2. Explain why advertisers make use of cartoon animals in their campaigns and how young children respond to them.
3. Explain what 'pester power' is and how advertisers make use of it.
4. How do young teens differ from younger children in the ways that they respond to advertisements?
5. By referring to the last two paragraphs, explain fully using your own words how the focus of an advertisement is shaped by an awareness of its audience's preferences and opinions.

EXTENSION

Do you think it is morally right or wrong to create adverts that are aimed at children?

Write an opinion piece in which you explain very clearly whether advertising to children as the target audience should be allowed.

Use the following paragraph planner to organise your thinking.

Paragraph	
1	Clearly state your perspective and the topic of your piece
2	Reason A, including development of the idea
3	Reason B, including development of the idea
4	Reason C, including development of the idea
5	Conclusion – summarise and express your perspective clearly and with force

LET'S TALK

As a class, discuss this question from Activity 5.1 again:

- Is your opinion of advertising positive, negative or neutral? What reasons and justifications can you give?

Have your opinions changed now that you have learned more about advertising techniques?

5 ADVERTISING

Writing and key skills

Creating your own advertisements

Activity 5.4

HINT
This decision may require compromise. In your group, before you discuss which option to choose, agree how to make the process fair for all members of the group, then decide on the product you will work on together. Work through your points of agreement and disagreement.

1 In a group of four or five, choose one of the following ideas for a product you will advertise:
   a Imagine that your school buildings and grounds are to be used as a luxury leisure centre for the public to use for short keep-fit health breaks.
   b Invent a lifestyle product that will be aimed at a certain target audience.
   c Choose an existing product, think of some improvements that could be made to it and advertise the new improved version.
2 As an advertising agency, you have been asked to create a:
   - single-page brochure
   - one-minute radio or podcast advert.

   You must think about:
   - target audience
   - branding
   - endorsement.
   - USP
   - lifestyle

   Use the prompts below to help you plan:
   - Remember that one of the skills of advertising is to make something that is quite mundane appear attractive and exciting so that people will want to buy it. (This might be particularly appropriate if you have chosen option a!)
   - Your brochure should include one or more slogans, one paragraph of detailed information designed to sell the lifestyle, and you should make clear decisions about the presentation.
   - Your radio advert should include a catchy jingle, public endorsements and clear information as well as persuasive techniques. Write a precise script and think carefully about the sentence types you will use.
   - Rehearse your radio script in your group. If possible, record yourselves and then play it back to decide on the improvements needed.
   - Use your imaginations and whatever ICT facilities you can that will help you to produce the glossiest brochure.

Speaking and listening

Performance

HINT
Consider how the different techniques used by performers have been effective in communicating the meaning and purpose of their piece.

Activity 5.5

When you have refined and developed your radio advert, perform it for the class, or play a recording that demonstrates the best version of your script.

As a class, listen to each other's work, and give positive and evaluative feedback, including suggestions for how it could be improved. Remember to consider the feelings of the performers.

Key skills

Figures of speech

Euphemisms

One of the skills of writing advertisements is to make something that is not very interesting, or perhaps even unpleasant, appear attractive and exciting so that potential customers will want to purchase it. To do this, advertising copywriters often **take some liberties** with language.

For example, think about the range of products now generally known as 'deodorants'. The purpose of a deodorant is to make a person smell attractive and, quite possibly, to hide more unpleasant smells such as dried sweat and so on. However, the advertising team that had to promote the first deodorants to the general public had a problem. A direct address to people saying, 'You smell, but use our product and you'll smell more pleasant' might well offend rather than appeal as most people do not like to be told that they smell! The problem lies in the word 'smell', which has unpleasant **connotations**. So, the advertisers searched for a word that meant something similar to 'smell' but – at the time – had more positive associations. They came up with the word 'odour'. It was apparently far less offensive to refer to people as having 'body odour' than to say that their bodies had a smell and so the term 'deodorant' was formed.

Disguising an unpleasant or offensive detail by substituting a more agreeable term is known as using a euphemism. We often use euphemisms; think, for example, of the terms we commonly use for dying or for death itself, such as 'pass away', 'breathe one's last' or 'eternal rest'.

Euphemisms are part of everyday English expression: being aware of their meanings will help you to speak and write effective **idiomatic** English.

> **WORD ATTACK SKILLS**
> Work out the meaning of the following words and phrases from the context of the lines in which they appear:
> ✔ take liberties
> ✔ connotations
> ✔ idiomatic

EXERCISE 5.5

1 Here is a list of euphemisms. Try to work out what they mean and who is likely to use them and in what situations.
   a armed intervention
   b challenging personality
   c correctional facility
   d powder one's nose
   e economical with the truth
   f smallest room in the house

2 Teachers sometimes use euphemisms when writing reports on students, especially for those whose behaviour is not as good as it should be. In the following report, the euphemistic phrases are underlined. Read it through and then write your own version, saying what you think the teacher really meant.

> Joe <u>needs to adopt a more focused approach</u> to his studies. He is <u>a lively member of the class</u> and <u>always expresses himself confidently and forcefully</u>. However, <u>he does not always accept authority easily</u> and <u>can be somewhat distracted</u> during lessons. He has <u>a good social network of friends and relates well to his peers, with whom he communicates regularly</u>. He has not yet <u>realised the importance of homework</u>. He has <u>a somewhat relaxed attitude to school</u> life and I suspect that <u>he is not working to his full potential</u>.

5 ADVERTISING

> **WORD ATTACK SKILLS**
> Work out the meaning of the following words and phrases from the context of the lines in which they appear.
> ✔ indefensible
> ✔ question-begging
> ✔ inflated
> ✔ insincerity

> **GLOSSARY**
> **cuttlefish** – a swimming mollusc with eight arms and two long tentacles

> **Author: Indira Gandhi**
> Indira Gandhi was the third prime minister of India and, to date, the only female person to hold the role. She was born in Prayagraj, India, in 1917, the daughter of the first prime minister of India. Ghandi served twice as prime minister: from 1966 to 1977 and from 1980 until 1984, when she was killed.

Harmless euphemisms?

In general, euphemisms are harmless and can be quite entertaining. However, in an essay written in 1946 called 'Politics and the English Language', George Orwell (who wrote the novel *1984*) argued that political speech and writing often communicate unpopular choices (the 'defence of the **indefensible**' as he puts it) and he wrote the following words of warning, which are still relevant today.

> Thus political language has to consist largely of euphemism, **question-begging** and sheer cloudy vagueness … The **inflated** style itself is a kind of euphemism. A mass of Latin words falls upon the facts like soft snow, blurring the outline and covering up all the details. The great enemy of clear language is **insincerity**. When there is a gap between one's real and one's declared aims, one turns as it were instinctively to long words and exhausted idioms, like a **cuttlefish** spurting out ink.

> **LET'S TALK**
> In a small group, discuss what point you think Orwell is making about political language. Do you agree with him? Can you think of any speeches or political writing that back up or contradict his point?

Below are two extracts from speeches of a similar educational theme, written almost forty years apart.

The first extract is from a speech given by Indira Gandhi, who was the third prime minister of India. She delivered her speech, 'What Educated Women Can Do', at the Golden Jubilee celebrations of the Indraprastha College for Women in 1974. Read an extract below.

Extract: 'What Educated Women Can Do'

Sometimes, I am very sad that even people who do science are quite unscientific in their thinking and in their other actions – not what they are doing in the laboratories but how they live at home or their attitudes towards other people. Now, for India to become what we want it to become with a modern, rational society and firmly based on what is good in our ancient tradition and in our soil, for this we have to have a thinking public, thinking young women who are not content to accept what comes from any part of the world but are willing to listen to it, to analyse it and to decide whether it is to be accepted or whether it is to be thrown out and this is the sort of education which we want, which enables our young people to adjust to this changing world and to be able to contribute to it.

Some people think that only by taking up very high jobs, you are doing something important or you are doing national service. But we all know that the most complex machinery will be ineffective if one small screw is not working as it should and that screw is just as important as any big part. It is the same in

Key skills

Author: Malala Yousafzai

Malala Yousafzai is a Pakistani activist who was shot by the Taliban (an Islamic political movement and military organisation based in Afghanistan) in 2012 because she demanded that girls should get an education. She survived and, in 2014, she became the youngest person to receive the Nobel Peace Prize. She continues to fight for girls' education.

> national life. There is no job that is too small; there is no person who is too small. Everybody has something to do. And if he or she does it well, then the country will run well.
>
> So, I hope that all of you who have this great advantage of education will not only do whatever work you are doing keeping the national interests in view, but you will make your own contribution to creating peace and harmony, to bringing beauty in the lives of our people and our country. I think this is the special responsibility of the women of India.
>
> Indira Ghandi

The second extract is from Malala Yousafzai's sixteenth-birthday speech at the United Nations, which she delivered in July 2013.

Extract: 'Education is the Only Solution'

Dear brothers and sisters, we want schools and education for every child's bright future. We will continue our journey to our destination of peace and education for everyone. No one can stop us. We will speak for our rights and we will bring change through our voice. We must believe in the power and the strength of our words. Our words can change the world.

Because we are all together, united for the cause of education. And if we want to achieve our goal, then let us empower ourselves with the weapon of knowledge and let us shield ourselves with unity and togetherness.

Dear brothers and sisters, we must not forget that millions of people are suffering from poverty, injustice and ignorance. We must not forget that millions of children are out of schools. We must not forget that our sisters and brothers are waiting for a bright peaceful future.

So let us wage a global struggle against illiteracy, poverty and terrorism and let us pick up our books and pens. They are our most powerful weapons.

One child, one teacher, one pen and one book can change the world.

Education is the only solution. Education first.

Malala Yousafzai

Activity 5.6

With a partner or a small group, read the two extracts above and discuss whether you think they agree with or contradict the point Orwell is making — do these speeches 'consist largely of euphemism, question-begging and sheer cloudy vagueness', or are they clear and to the point?

91

Reviewing

Reflect on your learning in this chapter.

Reading
- What did the extract 'Why advertisers target children' make you feel? Did it contain any ideas that were new to you?
- Has reading about literary devices in advertising affected your opinion about the industry and the way you might respond to advertising?
- How do you feel about the extract from 'Politics and the English Language'? Would you like to read more by George Orwell? Why?

Speaking and listening
- What speaking and listening skills did you develop during the course of this chapter? Are you able to listen to others and reconsider your opinion?
- Do you feel confident contributing in class discussions? Why? Why not?
- How did you feel before and after performing the radio advert?

Writing
- Writing an advert is very different from writing an essay or a story. Did you enjoy it? Were there any challenges?
- How did you choose to plan your writing? What are your preferred methods of planning?

Key skills
- How many new words have you added to your vocabulary? Try to list five or more.

Further reading
- 'Politics and the English Language' by George Orwell
- *No Logo* by Naomi Klein
- Adverts are everywhere. Next time you travel to school, look out for how many adverts you encounter on the way.

6 A good story

Reading
- Detective stories
- Scary stories
- A complete short story

Speaking and listening
- Group story-telling
- Discussing what makes a good story
- Listening to a story

A GOOD STORY

Writing
- A scene from a story – focus on character
- A start to a short story
- A summary of a plot

Key skills
- Synonyms and etymology

LET'S TALK
Work in a group of five or six to discuss these questions:
- Why are detectives so popular in fiction?
- Is it because the reader can get involved in the game of solving a mystery?
- Are they a form of escapism?
- What about scary stories, such as ghost stories? Why do or don't you enjoy them?
- Do you choose stories because you enjoy the genre, know the author or think the title is interesting?

6 A GOOD STORY

Speaking and listening

The best detectives are interesting characters …

Spotlight on: detectives in crime fiction

A key feature of crime fiction is the character of the detective who is responsible for solving the crimes. The character of the detective must be interesting. Detectives such as Miss Marple and Hercule Poirot (created by Agatha Christie), Sherlock Holmes (created by Sir Arthur Conan Doyle) and Mma Ramotswe (created by Alexander McCall Smith) have become world famous. Many TV crime series are built around the detective.

Manga comic books and anime films feature famous detectives, such as Detective Conan and Victorique. Their characters have been carefully created. For example, Conan is a young elementary school boy. He wears glasses and often a bow tie as well. He has a photographic memory and a good sense of humour. Victorique is a young girl with long blonde hair and is small and bossy, but she has an analytical mind which helps her to solve crimes.

HINT
Do an internet search to find out more about these characters.

DID YOU KNOW?
Manga are black and white comic-type books. Each book is one chapter or volume of a story.

Anime are movies or TV shows in full colour that feature characters like those in the manga books. Many famous manga characters are used in anime.

Activity 6.1

Manga and anime are very popular. With a partner, have a quick discussion about why you think people enjoy them so much.

- The drawings are brilliant!
- They don't just rely on language – everyone can enjoy them.
- The characters are well developed.
- The stories explore interesting topics.
- The stories are easy to follow.

Speaking and listening

Activity 6.2

Work in a pair or small group.

1. Create a manga detective character profile. You can draw your own character or base your ideas on one of the characters in the picture below. You can choose how to present your profile.
   - Give your character a name.
   - Describe how your character dresses and what they look like.
   - Describe how your character talks and moves.
   - Make notes about what makes this character a good detective. Think of adjectives that you could use to describe the character. Here are some ideas to start with:

meticulous	bossy	brave
analytical	skilful	tenacious
shrewd	eccentric	observant
clever	brilliant	quirky
inconspicuous	unconventional	

2. Show and describe the character you have created to the rest of the class.

3. Develop a scene in which you show how your character would react and what they would do when faced with a crime scene. For example, your character could be called to the scene of a burglary. They investigate and start looking for clues … and then it seems as if things are not as simple as they look.
   You can choose how to present your scene. You could sketch it and add speech bubbles or you could just write some notes and dialogue. Present your scene to another group.

6 A GOOD STORY

Reading

Detective stories

EXERCISE 6.1

The following extracts focus on the legendary Victorian private detective Sherlock Holmes, from the story 'The Speckled Band' and the contemporary (present day) Botswanan detective Mma Ramotswe, from the No. 1 Ladies' Detective Agency book *Tears of the Giraffe*. Both of these extracts are from the beginning of the story.

1. Read the two extracts carefully to get a general idea of the characters. Complete the Word attack skills on page 97 and look up the meaning of words you do not understand.

2. Read the extracts again and make a copy of the table below, in which you can add notes under the headings provided. This will help you to compare the characters. Some ideas have been included already.

	Sherlock Holmes	**Mma Ramotswe**
Nationality	British	Botswanan
How character speaks	Cheerily, soothingly 'Ha!'	Smiled, nodded head
Gestures	Pats arm of visitor (reassuring? patronising?)	Raises eyebrow (surprised?)
Actions	Orders coffee for visitor	Orders tea for visitor
Other	Keen observation Confident ('We shall soon set matters right, I have no doubt.')	Keen observation (observes the way other woman shakes hands) Empathy ('I am very sorry. I know what it is like to lose a child.') Honest ('I will not waste our time or your money.')

3. Share and discuss your notes with a partner or your group. Keep your notes for the exercise that follows.

> **DID YOU KNOW?**
> The crime writer Agatha Christie once said: 'Unless you are good at guessing, it is not much use being a detective.'

> **HINT**
> Look at the direct speech and the words the writers use to describe how the characters speak.

Extract: *The Adventures of Sherlock Holmes*

'Good morning, madam,' said Holmes cheerily. 'My name is Sherlock Holmes. This is my intimate friend and associate, Dr Watson, before whom you can speak as freely as before myself. Ha! I am glad to see that Mrs Hudson has had the good sense to light the fire. Pray draw up to it, and I shall order you a cup of hot coffee, for I observe that you are shivering.'

'It is not cold which makes me shiver,' said the woman in a low voice, changing her seat as requested.

Reading

WORD ATTACK SKILLS

Work out the meaning of the following words from your knowledge of word families and from the context in which the word is used:

- ✔ pitiable
- ✔ agitation
- ✔ premature
- ✔ all-comprehensive

'What, then?'

'It is fear, Mr Holmes. It is terror.' She raised her veil as she spoke, and we could see that she was indeed in a **pitiable** state of **agitation**, her face all drawn and grey, with restless frightened eyes, like those of some hunted animal. Her features and figure were those of a woman of thirty, but her hair was shot with **premature** grey, and her expression was weary and haggard. Sherlock Holmes ran her over with one of his quick, **all-comprehensive** glances.

'You must not fear,' said he soothingly, bending forward and patting her forearm. 'We shall soon set matters right, I have no doubt. You have come in by train this morning, I see.'

'You know me, then?'

'No, but I observe the second half of a return ticket in the palm of your left glove. You must have started early, and yet you had a good drive in a dog-cart, along heavy roads, before you reached the station.'

The lady gave a violent start and stared in bewilderment at my companion.

'There is no mystery, my dear madam,' said he, smiling. 'The left arm of your jacket is spattered with mud in no less than seven places. The marks are perfectly fresh. There is no vehicle save a dog-cart which throws up mud in that way, and then only when you sit on the left-hand side of the driver.'

'Whatever your reasons may be, you are perfectly correct,' said she. 'I started from home before six, reached Leatherhead at twenty past, and came in by the first train to Waterloo. Sir, I can stand this strain no longer; I shall go mad if it continues. I have no one to turn to – none, save only one, who cares for me, and he, poor fellow, can be of little aid. I have heard of you, Mr Holmes; I have heard of you from Mrs Farintosh, whom you helped in the hour of her sore need. It was from her that I had your address. Oh, sir, do you not think that you could help me, too, and at least throw a little light through the dense darkness which surrounds me? At present it is out of my power to reward you for your services, but in a month or six weeks I shall be married, with the control of my own income, and then at least you shall not find me ungrateful.'

Holmes turned to his desk and, unlocking it, drew out a small case-book, which he consulted.

'Farintosh,' said he. 'Ah yes, I recall the case; it was concerned with an **opal** tiara. I think it was before your time, Watson. I can only say, madam, that I shall be happy to devote the same care to your case as I did to that of your friend. As to reward, my profession is its own reward; but you are at liberty to **defray whatever expenses** I may be put to, at the time which suits you best. And now I beg that you will lay before us everything that may help us in forming an opinion upon the matter.'

Sir Arthur Conan Doyle

GLOSSARY

opal – a stone used in jewellery

defray expenses – to pay the costs of

6 A GOOD STORY

Extract: *Tears of the Giraffe*

The woman took her hand, correctly, Mma Ramotswe noticed, in the proper Botswana way, placing her left hand on her right forearm as a mark of respect. Most white people shook hands very rudely, snatching just one hand and leaving their other hand free to perform all sorts of mischief. This woman had at least learned something about how to behave.

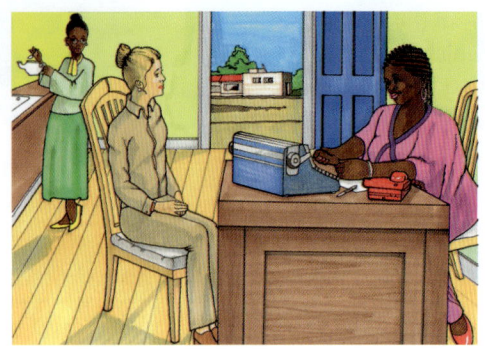

She invited the caller to sit down in the chair which they kept for clients, while Mma Makutsi busied herself with the kettle.

'I'm Mrs Andrea Curtin,' said the visitor. 'I heard from somebody in my embassy that you were a detective and you might be able to help me.'

Mma Ramotswe raised an eyebrow. 'Embassy?'

'The American Embassy,' said Mrs Curtin. 'I asked them to give me the name of a detective agency.'

Mma Ramotswe smiled. 'I am glad that they recommended me,' she said. 'But what do you need?'

The woman had folded her hands on her lap and now she looked down at them. The skin of her hands was mottled, Mma Ramotswe noticed, in the way that white people's hands were if they were exposed to too much sun. Perhaps she was an American who had lived for many years in Africa; there were many of these people. They grew to love Africa and they stayed, sometimes until they died. Mma Ramotswe could understand why they did this. She could not imagine why anybody would want to live anywhere else. How did people survive in cold, northern climates, with all that snow and rain and darkness?

'I could say that I am looking for somebody,' said Mrs Curtin, raising her eyes to meet Mma Ramotswe's gaze. 'But then that would suggest that there is somebody to look for. I don't think that there is so I suppose I should say that I'm trying to find out what happened to somebody, quite a long time ago. I don't expect that that person is alive. In fact, I am certain that he is not. But I want to find out what happened.'

Mma Ramotswe nodded. 'Sometimes it is important to know,' she said. 'And I am sorry, Mma, if you have lost somebody.'

Mrs Curtin smiled. 'You're very kind. Yes, I lost somebody.'

'When was this?' asked Mma Ramotswe.

'Ten years ago,' said Mrs Curtin. 'Ten years ago I lost my son.'

Reading

GLOSSARY

bush tea – herbal tea made from leaves of a red bush, also called rooibos or red bush tea

For a few moments there was a silence. Mma Ramotswe glanced over to where Mma Makutsi was standing near the sink and noticed that her secretary was watching Mrs Curtin attentively. When she caught her employer's gaze, Mma Makutsi looked guilty and returned to her task of filling the teapot.

Mma Ramotswe broke the silence. 'I am very sorry. I know what it is like to lose a child.'

'Do you, Mma?'

She was not sure whether the question had an edge to it, as if it were a challenge, but she answered gently. 'I lost my baby. He did not live.'

Mrs Curtin lowered her gaze. 'Then you know,' she said. Mma Makutsi had now prepared the **bush tea** and she brought over a chipped enamel tray on which two mugs were standing. Mrs Curtin took hers gratefully, and began to sip on the hot, red liquid.

'I should tell you something about myself,' said Mrs Curtin. 'Then you will know why I am here and why I would like you to help me. If you can help me I shall be very pleased, but if not, I shall understand.'

'I will tell you,' said Mma Ramotswe. 'I cannot help everybody. I will not waste our time or your money. I shall tell you whether I can help.'

Alexander McCall Smith

EXERCISE 6.2

Write a detailed comparison of the two passages. To do this you will need to look at the notes you made about each detective and then think about how these detective characters have been created by the writers.

In your comparison, focus on:
- the settings in which the scenes take place
- how the detectives behave and the ways in which they treat their clients
- how the grammatical features of their speech help to establish their individual characters
- the ways in which the writers introduce events, including the use of direct speech
- how you think that the stories may develop.

HINT

Refer closely to the passages in your answer. Quote words, phrases or sentences that support what you say. If, for example, you think that Sherlock Holmes is a confident character, you could support this by quoting: 'We shall soon set matters right, I have no doubt.'

Key skills

> **KEY WORD**
> **etymology** the origin of a word

Synonyms and etymology

You already know that different languages throughout history have influenced the development of English and contributed to modern English vocabulary.

One of the languages that has given a large number of words to English is Latin – the language spoken by the Romans 2000 years ago. However, many words that came from Latin did not enter English during the Roman occupation of Britain, which began in the days of the Emperor Claudius. These words became part of the language over 1000 years later during the historical period known as the Renaissance, when the revival of classical learning affected much of Europe. Legal and official documents at this time were written in Latin, which was the common language understood by educated people in different countries.

The English language absorbed words that came from Latin and used them alongside English words that already existed which had similar meanings. However, over the centuries, many Latin-derived words have acquired more formal and official associations than the equivalent words derived from Old English. Some of the original meanings have also changed or been lost over time.

For example, the adjective *cordial* comes from the Latin word *cor*, which means *heart*. The word *heart* derives from the Old English word *heort*. In Modern English, we can say that someone was given a *hearty* welcome and also that a person received a *cordial* welcome. However, although *hearty* and *cordial* have roots with a common meaning, their associations suggest a difference in warmth between the two types of welcome – a *hearty* welcome suggests a very warm and friendly reception whereas a *cordial* one suggests that, although perfectly friendly, the welcome consisted of little more than a polite handshake.

Being aware of such shades of meaning is a key skill in expressing yourself precisely in written and spoken English.

EXERCISE 6.3

1 Study the following Latin words and their meanings:
- *conspicere* – to look at attentively
- *amicus* – a friend; *amicabilis* – friendly
- *tenere* – to hold; *tenax* – clinging, holding fast
- *metus* – fear; *meticulosus* – fearful, timid
- *fors* – chance; *fortuitus* – happening by chance, accident
- *ante* – before; *antiquus* – ancient, former

2 Work out the meaning of the following English words.
- a inconspicuous
- b amicable
- c tenacious
- d fortuitous
- e antique
- f meticulous

Speaking and listening

3 Find a synonym for each of the words in Question 2 in the list below. Use each pair of words in sentences that show the slight differences in their meaning.
   a friendly
   b old
   c lucky
   d discreet
   e determined
   f fussy

Speaking and listening

What makes a good detective story?

GLOSSARY
red herring – a misleading clue

Crime fiction became very popular in the second half of the nineteenth century. Readers enjoyed stories with sinister and mysterious events, clever detectives, many suspects and ingenious, complicated plots (full of **red herrings**). Many of the stories also had an unexpected twist at the end, which led to the criminal finally being revealed.

Raymond Chandler (1888–1959) was an American author who created the private detective Philip Marlowe, who featured in books such as *Farewell, My Lovely* and *The Big Sleep*. He had some tips for writers of detective fiction. Here are a few of them:

> - It must be realistic in character, setting and atmosphere. It must be about real people in a real world.
> - It must have a sound story value apart from the mystery element: i.e. the investigation itself must be an adventure worth reading.
> - It must baffle a reasonably intelligent reader.
> - The solution must seem inevitable once revealed.
> - It must punish the criminal in one way or another, not necessarily by operation of the law … If the detective fails to resolve the consequences of the crime, the story is an unresolved chord and leaves irritation behind it.

Activity 6.3

Read Raymond Chandler's notes above and think about the detective characters you have read about and created. Then work in a pair to complete this activity.

Decide on a title for a short crime story that, between you, you will tell to the class.

Each of you will know only half of the story. One of you should prepare an account of what actually happened while the other prepares details of the place in which the event took place and the people involved. One of the characters should be a detective.

Toss a coin to decide which of you will start to tell the story. The first storyteller should begin and then, at a suitable point, pause to allow their partner to continue. Carry on taking turns until the story is finished. The whole activity should last about five minutes.

HINT
Each of you will need to adapt your version of events to match up with your partner's, as the story progresses.

Choose your words carefully and use gestures where you can to help bring the story to life.

6 A GOOD STORY

EXERCISE 6.4
Read the passage carefully. Complete the Word Attack Skills and look up the meaning of words you do not understand.

GLOSSARY
blotches – a stain or different coloured patch
yonder – over there
horde – (now spelt hoard) a collection of valued objects or money
harkened – listened (an old word not often in use nowadays)
staccato – short, sharp bursts (usually of sound)

Reading

Building suspense

Many readers enjoy scary stories. Horror stories about haunted houses and mysterious happenings have long been a feature of fiction writing. However, it is not just scary stories that use suspense to create tension. Good stories build suspense to draw the reader in – suspense can be used in any type of story writing, such as romance, science fiction, coming-of-age or historical fiction.

Beginning with suspense is a useful technique in story writing. The following passage is the opening to W.E.B. Du Bois's first fictional novel, *The Quest of the Silver Fleece*, published in 1911 and set in Alabama and Washington D.C.

Author: W.E.B. Du Bois

Du Bois (1868-1963) was an American sociologist, historian, author and activist. He was a prominent figure in the fight for racial justice in the early twentieth century. He was a prolific author and editor, and his essay collection, *The Souls of Black Folk*, is a cornerstone of African-American literature.

Extract: *The Quest of the Silver Fleece*

The Night fell. The red waters of the swamp grew sinister and **sullen**. The tall pines lost their slimness and stood in wide blurred **blotches** all across the way, and a great shadowy bird arose, wheeled and melted, murmuring, into the black-green sky.

The boy wearily dropped his heavy bundle and stood still, listening as the voice of crickets split the shadows and made the silence audible. A tear wandered down his brown cheek. They were at supper now, he whispered—the father and old mother, away back **yonder** beyond the night. They were far away; they would never be as near as once they had been, for he had stepped into the world. And the cat and Old Billy—ah, but the world was a lonely thing, so wide and tall and empty! And so bare, so bitter bare! Somehow he had never dreamed of the world as lonely before; he had fared forth to beckoning hands and luring, and to the eager hum of human voices, as of some great, swelling music.

Yet now he was alone; the empty night was closing all about him here in a strange land, and he was afraid. The bundle with his earthly treasure had hung heavy and heavier on his shoulder; his little **horde** of money was tightly wadded in his sock, and the school lay hidden somewhere far away in the shadows. He wondered how far it was; he looked and **harkened**, starting at his own heartbeats, and fearing more and more the long dark fingers of the night.

Then of a sudden up from the darkness came music. It was human music, but of a wildness and a weirdness that startled the boy as it fluttered and danced across the dull red waters of the swamp. He hesitated, then **impelled** by some strange power, left the highway and slipped into the forest of the swamp, shrinking, yet following the song hungrily and half forgetting his fear. A harsher, shriller note struck in as of many and ruder voices; but above it flew the first sweet music, birdlike, abandoned, and the boy crept closer.

Reading

The cabin crouched ragged and black at the edge of black waters. An old chimney leaned drunkenly against it, raging with fire and smoke, while through the chinks winked red gleams of warmth and wild cheer. With a revel of shouting and noise, the music suddenly ceased. Hoarse **staccato** cries and peals of laughter shook the old hut, and as the boy stood there peering through the black trees, abruptly the door flew open and a flood of light **illumined** the wood.

Amid this mighty halo, as on clouds of flame, a girl was dancing. She was black, and lithe, and tall, and willowy. Her garments twined and flew around the delicate moulding of her dark, young, limbs. A heavy mass of hair clung motionless to her wide forehead. Her arms twirled and flickered, and body and soul seemed quivering and whirring in the poetry of her motion.

As she danced she sang. He heard her voice as before, fluttering like a bird's in the full sweetness of her utter music. It was no tune nor melody, it was just formless, **boundless** music. The boy forgot himself and all the world besides. All his darkness was sudden light; dazzled he crept forward, bewildered, fascinated, until with one last wild whirl the elf-girl paused. The crimson light full upon the warm and velvet bronze of her face—her midnight eyes were aglow, her full purple lips apart, and all the music dead. **Involuntarily** the boy gave a gasping cry and awoke to swamp and night and fire, while a white face, drawn, red-eyed, peered outward from some hidden throng within the cabin.

'Who's that?' a harsh voice cried.

'Where?' 'Who is it?' and pale crowding faces blurred the light.

The boy wheeled blindly and fled in terror stumbling through the swamp, hearing strange sounds and feeling **stealthy** creeping hands and arms and whispering voices. On he toiled in mad haste, struggling toward the road and losing it until finally beneath the shadows of a mighty oak he sank exhausted. There he lay a while trembling and at last drifted into dreamless sleep.

W.E.B. Du Bois

WORD ATTACK SKILLS

Work out the meaning of the following words from the context of the lines in which they appear:

- ✓ sullen
- ✓ impelled
- ✓ illumined
- ✓ boundless
- ✓ involuntarily
- ✓ stealthy

EXERCISE 6.5

Write a summary of this passage in which you explain:
- what the narrator saw and heard
- what the narrator's thoughts and feelings were.

Write 150–200 words and use your own words as far as possible.

Activity 6.4

1. Work in a pair. Compare your summarised versions of the extract from *The Quest of the Silver Fleece* with the original passage. What has been lost by just concentrating on the facts contained in the original?
2. Discuss, with close reference to the original passage, how the author's description of the setting and the events that happen help to create suspense in the reader's mind.
   - What linking features does the writer use?
   - Does he use a variety of sentence types (simple, compound, complex) to create an effect?
   - Which words help to add suspense?
   - How does the author use punctuation to add meaning? Give an example.

6 A GOOD STORY

Reading and speaking

Short stories

Science fiction and fantasy can also be scary. Both are popular genres which appear as novels and short stories.

> **Spotlight on: short stories**
>
> Short stories, like other works of narrative fiction, have a theme, characters, setting and a plot. They usually provide a short and complete account of one scene or event. The plot is not as complex as that of a novel, although it has a conflict that is resolved at the end – often unexpectedly – with the twist. There are usually only a few characters, sometimes only one.

DID YOU KNOW?
The shortest short story is credited to Ernest Hemingway, who wrote the following:

For sale: baby shoes, never worn.

Author: Ray Bradbury

Ray Bradbury (1920-2012) was a celebrated twentieth-century American writer and screenwriter. He wrote works of fantasy, science fiction, horror, mystery and realistic fiction. His best known book is a novel called *Fahrenheit 451* (published in 1953) which is about a society in the future where books are forbidden.

KEY WORD
dystopian about an imaginary state or society in which there is suffering or injustice

EXERCISE 6.6

1. Before you read 'The Pedestrian', write a sentence or two in which you state your own opinion about science fiction and **dystopian** stories.
2. Then say if you think you will or will not enjoy the following dystopian short story by Ray Bradbury. Why or why not? Would your view be different if the title was different? How would you feel if it were called, for example, 'The arrest' or 'A walk'?
3. Read the story more than once to make sure you understand it. As you read, make short notes about the main character, the plot and the themes of the story.

The Pedestrian

To enter out into that silence that was the city at eight o'clock of a misty evening in November, to put your feet upon that buckling concrete walk, to step over grassy seams and make your way, hands in pockets, through the silences, that was what Mr Leonard Mead most dearly loved to do. He would stand upon the corner of an **intersection** and peer down long moonlit avenues of pavement in four directions, deciding which way to go, but it really made no difference; he was alone in this world of A.D. 2053, or as

good as alone, and with a final decision made, a path selected, he would stride off, sending patterns of frosty air before him like the smoke of a cigar.

Sometimes he would walk for hours and miles and return only at midnight to his house. And on his way he would see the cottages and homes with their dark windows, and it was not unequal to walking through a graveyard where only the faintest glimmers of firefly light appeared in flickers behind the windows. Sudden grey **phantoms** seemed to **manifest** upon inner room walls where a curtain was still undrawn against the night, or there were whisperings and murmurs where a window in a tomb-like building was still open.

Mr Leonard Mead would pause, cock his head, listen, look, and march on, his feet making no noise on the lumpy walk. For long ago he had wisely changed to sneakers when strolling at night, because the dogs in intermittent squads would parallel his journey with barkings if he wore hard heels, and lights might click on and faces appear and an entire street be startled by the passing of a lone figure, himself, in the early November evening.

On this particular evening he began his journey in a westerly direction, towards the hidden sea. There was a good crystal frost in the air; it cut the nose and made the lungs blaze like a Christmas tree inside; you could feel the cold light going on and off, all the branches filled with invisible snow. He listened to the faint push of his soft shoes through autumn leaves with satisfaction, and whistled a cold quiet whistle between his teeth, occasionally picking up a leaf as he passed, examining its skeletal pattern in the infrequent lamplights as he went on, smelling its rusty smell.

'Hello, in there,' he whispered to every house on every side as he moved. 'What's up tonight on Channel 4, Channel 7, Channel 9? Where are the cowboys rushing, and do I see the United States **Cavalry** over the next hill to the rescue?'

GLOSSARY
manifest – to become clear
Cavalry – soldier on horseback
scarab-beetles – large insects with hard, shell-like backs
phonograph – an old-fashioned machine for reproducing sound
riveted – fastened together with metal pins

6 A GOOD STORY

WORD ATTACK SKILLS

Work out the meaning of the following words from the context of the lines in which they appear:
- intersection
- phantoms
- puttering
- radiance
- ebbing

The street was silent and long and empty, with only his shadow moving like the shadow of a hawk in mid-country. If he closed his eyes and stood very still, frozen, he could imagine himself upon the centre of a plain, a wintry, windless Arizona desert with no house in a thousand miles, and only dry river beds, the streets, for company.

'What is it now?' he asked the houses, noticing his wrist watch. 'Eight-thirty p.m.? Time for a dozen assorted murders? A quiz? A revue? A comedian falling off the stage?'

Was that a murmur of laughter from within a moon-white house? He hesitated, but went on when nothing more happened. He stumbled over a particularly uneven section of pavement. The cement was vanishing under flowers and grass. In ten years of walking by night or day, for thousands of miles, he had never met another person walking, not one in all that time.

He came to a clover-leaf intersection which stood silent where two main highways crossed the town. During the day it was a thunderous surge of cars, the petrol stations open, a great insect rustling and a ceaseless jockeying for position as the **scarab-beetles**, a faint incense **puttering** from their exhausts, skimmed homeward to the far directions. But now these highways, too, were like streams in a dry season, all stone and bed and moon **radiance**.

He turned back on a side street, circling around towards his home. He was within a block of his destination when the lone car turned a corner quite suddenly and flashed a fierce white cone of light upon him. He stood entranced, not unlike a night moth, stunned by the illumination, and then drawn towards it.

A metallic voice called to him:

'Stand still. Stay where you are! Don't move!' He halted.

'Put up your hands!' 'But –' he said.

'Your hands up! Or we'll shoot!'

The police, of course, but what a rare, incredible thing; in a city of three million, there was only one police car left, wasn't that correct? Ever since a year ago, 2052, the election year, the force had been cut down from three cars to one. Crime was **ebbing**; there was no need now for the police, save for this one lone car wandering and wandering the empty streets.

'Your name?' said the police car in a metallic whisper. He couldn't see the men in it for the bright light in his eyes.

'Leonard Mead,' he said.

'Speak up!'

'Leonard Mead!'

'Business or profession?'

'I guess you'd call me a writer.'

'No profession,' said the police car, as if talking to itself. The light held him fixed, like a museum specimen, needle thrust through the chest.

'You might say that,' said Mr Mead. He hadn't written in years. Magazines and books didn't sell any more. Everything went on in the tomb-like houses at night now, he thought, continuing his fancy. The tombs, ill-lit by television light, where the people sat like the dead, the grey or multi-coloured lights touching their faces, but never really touching them.

'No profession,' said the **phonograph** voice, hissing. 'What are you doing out?'

'Walking,' said Leonard Mead.

'Walking!'

'Just walking,' he said simply, but his face felt cold.

'Walking, just walking, walking?'

'Yes, sir.'

'Walking where? For what?'

'Walking for air. Walking to see.'

'Your address!'

'Eleven South Saint James Street.'

'And there is air in your house, you have an air conditioner, Mr Mead?'

'Yes.'

'And you have a viewing screen in your house to see with?'

'No.'

'No?' There was a crackling quiet that in itself was an accusation.

'Are you married, Mr Mead?'

'No.'

'Not married,' said the police voice behind the fiery beam. The moon was high and clear among the stars and the houses were grey and silent.

'Nobody wanted me,' said Leonard Mead with a smile.

'Don't speak unless you're spoken to!'

Leonard Mead waited in the cold night.

'Just walking, Mr Mead?'

'Yes.'

'But you haven't explained for what purpose.'

'I explained; for air, and to see, and just to walk.'

'Have you done this often?'

'Every night for years.'

The police car sat in the centre of the street with its radio throat faintly humming.

'Well, Mr Mead,' it said.

'Is that all?' he asked politely.

'Yes,' said the voice. 'Here.' There was a sigh, a pop. The back door of the police car sprang wide.

'Get in.'

'Wait a minute, I haven't done anything!'

'Get in.'

'I protest!'

'Mr Mead.'

He walked like a man suddenly drunk. As he passed the front window of the car he looked in. As he had expected, there was no-one in the front seat, no-one in the car at all.

'Get in.'

He put his hand to the door and peered into the back seat, which was a little cell, a little black jail with bars. It smelled of **riveted** steel. It smelled of harsh antiseptic; it smelled too clean and hard and metallic. There was nothing soft there.

'Now if you had a wife to give you an alibi,' said the iron voice. 'But – '

'Where are you taking me?'

The car hesitated, or rather gave a faint whirring click, as if information, somewhere, was dropping card by punch-slotted card under electric eyes. 'To the Psychiatric Centre for Research on Regressive Tendencies.'

He got in. The door shut with a soft thud. The police car rolled through the night avenues, flashing its dim lights ahead.

They passed one house on one street a moment later, one house in an entire city of houses that were dark, but this one particular house had all of its electric lights brightly lit, every window a loud yellow illumination, square and warm in the cool darkness.

'That's my house,' said Leonard Mead.

No-one answered him.

The car moved down the empty river-bed streets and off away, leaving the empty streets with the empty pavements, and no sound and no motion all the rest of the chill November night.

Ray Bradbury

Writing

Activity 6.5

Analyse the story you have read by discussing the following questions in a group. Make notes of your answers so that you can share these with the rest of the class later.

1. What is this story about? Give a brief description.
2. What do you learn about the character of Leonard Mead? Do you like him and identify with him? Does this affect your view of the story?
3. In what way could this story be called dystopian?
4. What mood or atmosphere does the writer create in the story? Find words and phrases from the story to support your ideas.
5. What image does the writer use in the following lines? What effect does this have?

   'Everything went on in the tomb-like houses at night now, he thought, continuing his fancy. The tombs, ill-lit by television light, where the people sat like the dead, ...'
6. What do you think the main theme or themes of this story are?
7. Have you read any other stories or novels with similar themes? How were they similar or different?

Writing

A short story

HINTS
- The tone and register of your writing must be appropriate for its purpose.
- Use dialogue (direct speech) to develop your characters and scenes. You can use non-standard English in the dialogue if this helps to develop a character.
- Ensure that your handwriting is legible.

Activity 6.6

1. Write the opening scenes of a detective or short scary story in which you set the scene and introduce the main character(s). You should not aim to complete the whole story but should concentrate on creating a convincing and mysterious scenario. Think about the mood and tone, and words you will need to describe this. Also think about the punctuation you could use to enhance the feeling of mystery and suspense. Your opening should be about 200 words.

   Here are a few ideas you could use or adapt:

   Maya began to realise what the expression spine-chilling meant ... a shiver ran down her spine ... but she determined to carry on.

   Why was there a rabbit on the bathroom floor?

   The lights flickered, there was a loud BANG! And everything went dark.

2. Read the opening to a partner or your group. Discuss how the story could continue and what you would need to do to make it interesting for the reader.

EXTENSION

Use your opening scene from Activity 6.6 or any other ideas to write a complete short story of 600–800 words.

6 A GOOD STORY

Reviewing
Reflect on your learning in this chapter.

Reading
- Which text did you find most engaging and why?
- Did you enjoy the detective stories? Why? Would you like to read other detective stories or novels?
- Would you recommend reading ghost stories to a friend? Why?
- How do you feel about reading aloud? Has your confidence grown this year?

Speaking and listening
- What speaking and listening skills did you develop during this chapter?
- Does it help to share your ideas with a group or a partner? Why?
- How comfortable did you feel working in a group?

Writing
- Do you enjoy writing? Are there any parts of the process you particularly enjoy or find challenging?
- Did you choose to write a detective story or a scary story? Why?
- Which literary devices did you use in your story?

Key skills
- Pick the five new words you have learned in this chapter that you found most interesting.
- Define 'synonym'.
- Do you find etymology interesting? Does it help you to decipher the meaning of new words?

Further reading
If you enjoyed reading these extracts, you might enjoy:
- 'The Dinner Party' by Mona Gardner (you can find this online)
- 'Girl' by Jamaica Kincaid
- *The Adventures of Sherlock Holmes* by Arthur Conan Doyle
- *Fake ID* by Lamar Giles
- *Dread Nation* by Justina Ireland

7 Exploring complex themes

Reading
- Themes in poems
- A Shakespeare tragedy play

Speaking and listening
- A class discussion about themes
- Listening to a poem
- A group discussion about pride
- A performance of *Romeo and Juliet*
- Giving and receiving constructive feedback

Writing
- An autobiographical piece about a time when pride affected you
- A poem about behaviour and feelings
- A story about a time when loyalty led to a problem
- The writing process

Key skills
- Iambic pentameter

EXPLORING COMPLEX THEMES

LET'S TALK

As a class, discuss what you know about themes in writing.
- Name some themes.
- List some poems or stories that have strong themes.
- Talk about literary devices and techniques writers use to present a theme.

7 EXPLORING COMPLEX THEMES

Reading

Exploring themes

Poet: Percy Shelley

Born in 1792, Percy Bysshe Shelley was a nineteenth-century poet. He was part of the Romantic movement, which emphasised the relationship between humans and their emotions and the natural world.

Activity 7.1

Work with a partner. Take it in turns to read the poem out loud, then listen to a recording of the poem. Discuss how it is different to the way you both read it and how listening to poems aids your understanding of them.

WORD ATTACK SKILLS

Which words or phrases made you stumble when you read the poem out loud?

What aspects of the poem first struck you as you read it or listened to it being read?

Write your own, or research, definitions of these words from the poem:

- ✔ vast
- ✔ visage
- ✔ sneer
- ✔ mocked
- ✔ pedestal
- ✔ mighty
- ✔ decay
- ✔ colossal
- ✔ boundless

'Ozymandias'

I met a traveller from an antique land,
Who said: 'Two **vast** and trunkless legs of stone
Stand in the desert … Near them, on the sand,
Half sunk, a shattered **visage** lies, whose frown,
And wrinkled lip, and **sneer** of cold command,
Tell that its sculptor well those passions read
Which yet survive, stamped on these lifeless things,
The hand that **mocked** them, and the heart that fed;
And on the **pedestal**, these words appear:
My name is Ozymandias, King of Kings;
Look on my Works, ye **Mighty**, and despair!
Nothing beside remains. Round the **decay**
Of that **colossal** Wreck, **boundless** and bare
The lone and level sands stretch far away.'

Percy Shelley

Reading

Activity 7.2

Spotlight on: poetic form

The poem is a sonnet, which means there are only 14 lines for the poet to use to explore the theme of the poem. Despite this, Shelley has seemingly given up the first line, just to introduce the traveller: 'I met a traveller from an antique land'.

1 Why do you think Shelley chose to use the line in this way?
2 Do you think the line could be put to better use?
3 What effect does this line have on the meaning of the poem, or on you as the reader?

EXERCISE 7.1

Not many of us will grow up to be as powerful as Ozymandias once was, or have a giant statue built in our honour. However, we can still relate to the poem and explore its themes in relation to our own personal life and experience. Spend some time reflecting and making notes on the theme of pride.

1 With your partner, discuss which of these themes best apply to the poem:
   - Betrayal
   - Environment
   - Growing up
   - Power
   - Friendship
   - Justice
   - Family
   - Pride
   - Poverty

   Choose appropriate words or phrases from the poem that support and justify your choices.

2 Choose from the following options. Which best interpret the meaning of the poem?
   A The poem is mostly spoken by a traveller to an ancient, ruined country.
   B The poet tells a story to a traveller about an antique object.
   C The traveller has strong legs but has lost some luggage.
   D There is a giant, ruined statue which has partly collapsed.
   E The face of the traveller has been damaged so he lies on the sand.
   F The head of the statue has fallen and lies on the ground next to the legs.
   G The face of the statue looks proud and powerful.
   H The face of the statue is stone so it is cold to touch.
   I The statue is of an ancient king called Ozymandias.
   J The traveller turns out to be a king called Ozymandias.
   K The statue's inscription shows how the ruler despaired because he could not rule for ever.
   L The statue's inscription was supposed to show the eternal power of the ruler.
   M The statue now shows how power can be taken away and mean nothing.
   N The statue now shows that power can still be important in the desert.

3 The poem contains some memorable phrases.
   a 'sneer of cold command'
   This phrase describes the expression on the statue's face. Imagine the king in person. Describe the personality that you associate with this image. What character traits would you expect the king to have, based on this simple phrase?
   b 'Look on my works, ye Mighty, and despair!'
   This phrase is the heart of the poem. It has been written as an inscription to boast of the achievements of the great King Ozymandias. Explain fully how this phrase contains the central message of the poem.
   c 'The lone and level sands stretch far away.'
   The poet chooses to end the poem with this descriptive phrase. How would you choose to perform this line? Explain fully how your performance choice would match the purpose of this phrase in relation to the meaning of the poem as a whole.

7 EXPLORING COMPLEX THEMES

Writing

Pride

> **LET'S TALK**
>
> Pride has both positive and negative associations:
> - A parent or teacher may say 'I am proud of you' or 'You should be proud of yourself'.
> - On the other hand, there is an old-fashioned saying: 'Pride comes before a fall.'
>
> In a group of five or six, discuss what thoughts you have about pride. Is it a positive force in your life? Or does it sometimes have a negative impact?

EXERCISE 7.2

Write an autobiographical piece about a time when pride (or its opposite) affected you.

You may choose not to plan your writing in a structured way. Writing can be a way to explore a feeling or memory, without knowing fully where the first sentence will take you.

> **HINT**
>
> When writing about personal experience, you need to think about the following, which will affect how you use language.
> - When you write about your own past, one memory can awaken another memory, then another, then another … and so on. Your sentence structure can reflect this, by including compound and complex sentences.
> - An autobiographical reflection will shift between descriptive details and emotional responses. Your choices about whether to write formally or informally will affect how you manage this.
> - You may include dialogue or brief bits of speech but they should not overtake the text. You are not writing a story.
> - You will use the past tense to describe the past events, but you may switch to present tense in places, as the current 'you' reflects on the past 'you'.

Reading

Exploring themes

The poem on page 115, by Stevie Smith, uses a quiet, ironic voice to tackle the themes of personality and the puzzle of how our behaviour does not always show our deepest feelings.

Writing

Author: Stevie Smith

Stevie Smith was born in England in 1902. Her poems often sounded like children's songs or nursery rhymes and were sometimes accompanied by simple, cartoon-like drawings. However, the poetry was deceptive – underneath the surface there was a poet of great skill, with a surprising and deadly sense of humour. She died in 1971.

'Not Waving but Drowning'

Nobody heard him, the dead man,
But still he lay moaning:
I was much further out than you thought
And not waving but drowning.

Poor chap, he always loved larking
And now he's dead
It must have been too cold for him his heart gave way,
They said.

Oh, no no no, it was too cold always
(Still the dead one lay moaning)
I was much too far out all my life
And not waving but drowning.

Stevie Smith

WORD ATTACK SKILLS

The word 'larking' is slightly old-fashioned and means to play about or to be slightly silly in a jokey, physical way.

What phrases and words do you use in school and at home for this sort of behaviour?

Here are some synonyms and connected words, some of which are rarely used in modern English. These verbs have a similar meaning to 'larking':

- ✔ romping
- ✔ gambolling

These adjectives could be used to describe someone who is larking about:

- ✔ rollicking
- ✔ rambunctious
- ✔ rumbustious
- ✔ exuberant

Try using these words in sentences of your own.

Enjoy the music of these unusual words. Read them aloud to share with the class.

7 EXPLORING COMPLEX THEMES

> **Activity 7.3**
>
> 1 The line 'And not waving but drowning' is repeated in the poem, but it has two different meanings. Explain these two different meanings: one is literal, the other is a metaphor.
> 2 The poet repeats another line with a slight variation:
>
> > I was much further out than you thought
> > I was much too far out all my life
>
> Again – explain the literal, and then the metaphorical meaning of these lines.
>
> 3 Explore the poem for other repeated images or phrases. How do these repetitions build up the meaning and personality of the main character who forms the subject of the poem?

> **Spotlight on: poetic techniques**
>
> Although the poem appears simple, with a simple rhyme pattern, it uses some advanced techniques that show Stevie Smith's skill as a poet.
>
> Despite seeming like ordinary speech, there is a music to the rhythm of the words. Look at the first two lines, for example:
>
> > Nobody heard him, the dead man,
> > But still he lay moaning:
>
> Say these lines out loud with a partner. Tap out the rhythm with your fingertips. Listen for the music of the lines, and continue your reading of the poem with the sense of rhythm. Notice how it flows in some places but then stops suddenly in others.
>
> In particular, look for the following techniques:
> - enjambment – where the end of the line is not the end of the sentence, and may not require a pause
> - end-stopping – lines that pause or have a punctuation mark at the end are called 'end-stopped'
> - **caesura** – a pause or break in the middle of a line.
>
> What interests or puzzles you about the line endings? How has Stevie Smith used certain line endings to draw attention to certain words or phrases?
>
> How does the use of caesura draw our attention to certain ideas or key words and phrases?

> **KEY WORD**
>
> **caesura** a pause or break in the middle of a line

Writing

Creating your own poem

In the poem, Stevie Smith explores the difference between the behaviour someone displays and the feelings this may hide.

Your task is to explore this through writing your own poem using this theme.

> **HINT**
> As you write your poem, think about the lines, rather than the sentences.
>
> Have you thought about using **antithesis** in your poem?

> **KEY WORD**
> **antithesis** a technique used in poetry and other forms of writing, which compares or connects opposites. In Stevie Smith's poem, she uses subtle versions of antithesis throughout. The opposites are not obvious opposites, but they are there. For example, the impossibility of a dead man 'moaning' is an example of this technique being used very carefully

EXERCISE 7.3

Planning stage 1 – initial ideas

Use the following prompts to help think of an initial idea.
- Do you ever behave in a way that hides your feelings?
- Do you know anyone who pretends to be full of confidence but is in fact shy or worried?
- Why do people often hide their feelings? Is it always to keep secrets?

Now make a list of some opposite feelings and behaviours.

Planning stage 2 – jotting down some beginnings

A poet looks incredibly closely at the subject, even if it is in their imagination.

Picture your main character, the subject of your poem. It may be a version of you, or someone completely different. Look as closely as you can.

Jot down some phrases or words to describe anything and everything about them:
- appearance
- habits
- hopes, fears, dreams
- movements
- way of talking
- ...
- facial expressions

At this stage, do not worry about being 'poetic'. You do not need to use clever words or techniques, just let the ideas flow onto the page to bring the image into closer and closer focus.

7 EXPLORING COMPLEX THEMES

Planning stage 3 – choosing your starting point

Look through the notes you have made.
- Choose a phrase, word or image that catches your attention.
- Turn the phrase, word or image into a sentence that describes the subject of your poem – the character.
- Now play with that sentence:
  - Try changing the tense.
  - Add a clause with some descriptive detail.
  - Write a negative version of the sentence (antithesis).
  - Try writing the sentence in a different order.
  - Keep playing until you have a sentence that interests you.

This sentence will be the starting point for your writing.

Writing your poem

Remember, the theme of your poem is about how behaviour does not always show our feelings.

Work from your starting point – the sentence you created in planning stage 3. Write sentences that interest you, and try variations like you did in the planning stage. When you have three or four sentences, you can start forming them into a poem.

Your poem does not need to rhyme, but think carefully about the pauses in your poem. Some lines will be end-stopped, but others may flow on, using enjambment, or have a break in the middle, using caesura. You will need to make decisions based on the rhythm of your words, but also according to which words you want to stand out more brightly than others.

Review and revise

When you have built your poem, create a working draft to share with a partner.

Take it in turns to read your poems, and to ask questions.

Has the poem painted a vivid picture of the subject: someone whose behaviour and feelings do not quite match?

Reading

Who was Shakespeare?

William Shakespeare was born in the Warwickshire town of Stratford-upon-Avon. His date of birth is generally considered to have been 23 April 1564 and it is believed that he died, also in Stratford, on his birthday in 1616. For someone so famous, whose works are so well known, the precise details of his life are quite limited. We know that he was at school in Stratford and that his father was a merchant in the town (and later was awarded his own coat of arms, which was a sign of status). We know that Shakespeare did not attend university and that he married a woman called Anne Hathaway who came from a village near Stratford and who was seven years older than him. They had three children but the direct line of Shakespeare's descendants died out after two generations.

Shakespeare, however, did not spend all his life in Stratford. At some point during the 1590s he moved to London (leaving his wife and family in Stratford) and became involved in the theatrical scene in the capital. He worked as an actor in one of the theatre companies, The Lord Chamberlain's Men, and increasingly as a dramatist writing plays for them.

◂ A typical Elizabethan theatre

Why Shakespeare is still relevant today

Another great dramatist of the time, Ben Jonson, was both a friend and a rival of Shakespeare. He wrote that Shakespeare 'was not of an age, but for all time' and over the centuries Jonson's judgement has proved true. What makes Shakespeare so great a writer and so relevant to audiences of all periods is a combination of the force of his poetry, his technical skill as a writer for the theatre, the wealth and variety of the true-to-life characters he created and the universality of the themes of his plays.

The themes of his play cover the deepest of human experience: love, loss, betrayal, war, fear, anger, revenge, hope, enslavement, jealousy, politics, power, … the list goes on and on.

Look for the major themes packed into the short extract below as you read it.

▲ From a Royal Shakespeare Company production of *Hamlet*

An example of Shakespeare's dramatic writing

Here is an extract from one of Shakespeare's plays for you to enjoy and to test your understanding. It is taken from *Romeo and Juliet*, a play set in Verona in Italy. Two of the leading families of the city, the Montagues and the Capulets, have been engaged in a feud (a bitter quarrel) for generations. In this scene, Romeo, a Montague, has gone with his friend Benvolio to a masked ball at the Capulet house. He is recognised by Tybalt, one of the Capulet family, who is furious that a Montague should have gatecrashed this party and tells Old Capulet, the head of the family. Romeo, who does not realise that he has been recognised, is preoccupied

Reading

with the beauty of Juliet, whom he sees for the first time. He is not aware that she is Capulet's daughter, and he approaches her to declare his love for her.

The play was written to be watched, not read, so try to watch a version of the scene being acted. There are many film and stage versions. One famous film adaptation was directed by Baz Luhrmann in 1996 and starred Claire Danes as Juliet and Leonardo Di Caprio as Romeo.

Follow the scene carefully and then answer the questions on page 124. The words that are highlighted are explained to the right of the text.

▲ Romeo and Juliet meet

Extract: *Romeo and Juliet* Act 1 Scene 5

Romeo: [*To a Servingman*] What lady is that, which doth enrich the hand
Of **yonder** knight?   at some distance; 'over there'

Servant: I know not, sir.

Romeo: O, she doth teach the torches to burn bright!
It seems she hangs upon the cheek of night
Like a rich jewel in an Ethiope's ear;
Beauty too rich for use, for earth too dear!
So shows a snowy dove trooping with crows,
As yonder lady o'er her fellows shows.
The measure done, I'll watch her place of stand,
And, touching hers, make blessed my rude hand.

7 EXPLORING COMPLEX THEMES

	Did my heart love till now? **forswear** it, sight!	give up or let go of
	For I ne'er saw true beauty till this night.	
Tybalt:	This, by his voice, should be a Montague.	
	Fetch me my **rapier**, boy. What dares the slave	a type of sword
	Come hither, cover'd with an antic face,	
	To **fleer** and scorn at our solemnity?	laugh at
	Now, by the stock and honour of my kin,	
	To strike him dead, I hold it not a sin.	
Capulet:	Why, how now, kinsman! **wherefore** storm you so?	why
Tybalt:	Uncle, this is a Montague, our foe,	
	A villain that is **hither** come in spite,	to this place, to here
	To scorn at our **solemnity** this night.	serious feeling or behaviour
Capulet:	Young Romeo is it?	
Tybalt:	'Tis he, that villain Romeo.	
Capulet:	Content thee, gentle **coz**, let him alone;	cousin
	He bears him like a portly gentleman;	
	And, to say truth, Verona brags of him	
	To be a virtuous and well-govern'd youth:	
	I would not for the wealth of all the town	
	Here in my house do him **disparagement**:	to talk of as of little value; to belittle
	Therefore be patient, take no note of him:	
	It is my will, the which if thou respect,	
	Show a fair presence and put off these frowns,	
	An ill-beseeming **semblance** for a feast.	appearance
Tybalt:	It fits, when such a villain is a guest:	
	I'll not **endure** him.	tolerate
Capulet:	He shall be endured:	
	What, goodman boy! I say, he shall: go to;	
	Am I the master here, or you? Go to.	
	You'll not endure him! God shall mend my soul!	
	You'll make a mutiny among my guests!	
	You will set cock-a-hoop! You'll be the man!	
Tybalt:	Why, uncle, 'tis a shame.	
Capulet:	Go to, go to;	
	You are a saucy boy: is't so, indeed?	
	This trick may chance to scathe you, I know what:	
	You must contrary me! Marry, 'tis time. [*To dancers nearby.*]	
	Well said, my hearts! You are a princox; go:	
	Be quiet, or – [*To the Servants.*] More light, more light!	
	For shame!	
	I'll make you quiet. [*To dancers.*] What, cheerly, my hearts!	

Tybalt:	Patience perforce with wilful **choler** meeting	anger
	Makes my flesh tremble in their different greeting.	
	I will withdraw: but this intrusion shall	
	Now seeming sweet convert to bitter **gall**.	foul tasting digestive liquid. Used metaphorically
Exit		
Romeo:	[*To Juliet*] If I **profane** with my unworthiest hand	show disrespect to
	This holy shrine, the gentle fine is this:	
	My lips, two blushing pilgrims, ready stand	
	To smooth that rough touch with a tender kiss.	
Juliet:	Good **pilgrim**, you do wrong your hand too much,	a person making a religious journey
	Which mannerly devotion shows in this;	
	For saints have hands that pilgrims' hands do touch,	
	And **palm to palm is holy palmers' kiss**.	holding palms together is like a pilgrim's kiss
Romeo:	Have not saints lips, and holy palmers too?	
Juliet:	Ay, pilgrim, lips that they must use in prayer.	
Romeo:	O, then, dear saint, let lips do what hands do;	
	They pray, **grant** thou, lest faith turn to despair.	allow or agree
Juliet:	Saints do not move, though grant for prayers' sake.	
Romeo:	Then move not, while my prayer's effect I take.	
	Thus from my lips, by yours, my sin is purged.	
Juliet:	Then have my lips the sin that they have took.	
Romeo:	Sin from thy lips? O **trespass** sweetly urged!	allow or agree
	Give me my sin again.	
Juliet:	You kiss by the book.	
Nurse:	Madam, your mother craves a word with you.	
Romeo:	What is her mother?	
Nurse:	Marry, bachelor,	
	Her mother is the lady of the house,	
	And a good lady, and a wise and virtuous	
	I nursed her daughter, that you talk'd withal;	
	I tell you, he that can lay hold of her	
	Shall have the **chinks**.	wealth
Romeo:	Is she a Capulet?	
	O dear account! my life is my foe's debt.	
Benvolio:	Away, begone; the sport is at the best.	
Romeo:	Ay, so I fear; the more is my unrest.	
Capulet:	Nay, gentlemen, prepare not to be gone;	
	We have a **trifling** foolish banquet towards.	silly
	Is it e'en so? Why, then, I thank you all	

7 EXPLORING COMPLEX THEMES

> I thank you, honest gentlemen; good night.
> More torches here! Come on then, let's to bed.
> Ah, sirrah, **by my fay**, it waxes late: upon my word; I swear
> I'll to my rest.
>
> *Exeunt all but* Juliet *and* Nurse.
>
> Juliet: Come hither, nurse. What is yond gentleman?
> Nurse: The son and heir of old Tiberio.
> Juliet: What's he that now is going out of door?
> Nurse: Marry, that, I think, be young Petrucio.
> Juliet: What's he that follows there, that would not dance?
> Nurse: I know not.
> Juliet: Go ask his name: if he be married.
>   My grave is like to be my wedding bed.
> Nurse: His name is Romeo, and a Montague;
>   The only son of your great enemy.
> Juliet: My only love sprung from my only hate!
>   Too early seen unknown, and known too late!
>   Prodigious birth of love it is to me,
>   That I must love a loathed enemy.

EXERCISE 7.4

1. Look at Romeo's first speech, beginning 'O, she doth teach the torches …', and explore how the similes and metaphors he uses show how he sees Juliet's beauty.
2. Imagine this scene in performance. Explain as fully as you can the ways in which Tybalt's reaction to Romeo's presence add to the tension in the scene.
3. Explain as fully as you can the difference in the behaviour of Tybalt and Old Capulet. Why do you think that Old Capulet behaves as he does? You should refer to the text in your answer.
4. When he first speaks to Juliet, Romeo asks if he may kiss her. Explain the metaphor in the first four lines of his speech. What does the language he uses suggest about Romeo's character?
5. How does Juliet respond?
6. Look closely at the dialogue between Romeo and Juliet from 'If I profane …' to '… my prayer's effect I take.' What do you notice about the poetic form of these lines and what effect does this create?
7. What impression do you have of Juliet's nurse from what she says and does in this scene?
8. Juliet asks the nurse, 'What is yond gentleman?' Why do you think the nurse does not immediately refer to Romeo in her reply?
9. Explain in your own words Juliet's four lines at the end of the scene, beginning 'My only love sprung from my only hate!'
10. By referring to what people say and do throughout this scene, explain fully what you have learned about the society of Verona, the feud between the two families, your thoughts about the relationship between Romeo and Juliet and what you learn about social attitudes in a different historical culture.

Key skills

Iambic pentameter

> **KEY WORD**
> **iambic pentameter**
> a line of ten syllables (or five iambic feet). Each iambic foot is composed of an unstressed syllable followed by a stressed syllable

Shakespeare's plays are written in what is known as blank verse or unrhymed **iambic pentameters**. A pentameter is simply a line of verse containing five 'feet', each containing two syllables (so that there are ten syllables in total). For example:

'If music be the food of love, play on'

(This is the opening line of *Twelfth Night*.) An iambus is the name given to a verse 'foot' which contains an unstressed syllable followed by a stressed syllable, as in the example:

'If mu/sic be/ the food/ of love/, play on'

The iambic meter closely reflects the rhythms of ordinary English speech. Shakespeare's iambic pentameters do not usually rhyme although he often uses a rhyme to indicate the end of a scene or to communicate a memorable series of thoughts. Although most of the verse in all of Shakespeare's plays is in iambic pentameter, there are often small changes in the pattern so that the language does not become monotonous.

Read through some of the speeches by Tybalt, Capulet, Juliet or Romeo. Count the syllables and tap the rhythms on your fingers.

Speaking and listening

Translating to modern English

Though Shakespeare is still relevant today, and has proven to be 'for all time', lots of dramatists have 'translated' his plays into modern English, in part to make them more accessible, particularly for younger audiences.

7 EXPLORING COMPLEX THEMES

> **Activity 7.4**
>
> In a group of five, turn the scene into modern English, then perform your version of the scene to the rest of your class.
>
> Do not try to translate word-for-word, but instead show the following characteristics and behaviour:
>
>
>
> ▲ Tybalt's anger at Romeo's presence
>
> ▲ Capulet's ability to control Tybalt's behaviour but not how he feels
>
>
>
> ▲ Romeo and Juliet's innocent and joyful love-at-first-sight
>
> ▲ The nurse's anxiety for Juliet – trying to prevent her getting in trouble
>
> Your scene could be set at a school disco, or in another modern setting.
>
> Think about how to use different dramatic techniques including stage directions to develop the meaning of the text.

Writing

A test of loyalty

The theme of loyalty recurs often in Shakespeare's plays – and indeed in many plays going all the way back to the Ancient Greeks. Loyalty is still the subject of present-day dramas.

> **EXERCISE 7.5**
>
> You are going to write a story about a time when loyalty to a friend led to a problem.
>
> 1 You should first decide whether to tell the story in the first or third person. Both can be equally effective; a first-person narrative may make personal reflection and maybe a sense of remorse about the episode more direct, but a third-person approach may make it easier to write an objective analysis of the episode. The choice is yours.

2   When writing a short story of any kind, you will need to consider the following:
- Make sure that you write an opening paragraph that will immediately capture the reader's attention; you're writing a short story so every paragraph is important to its development. One way of doing this is by starting with a direct question such as 'Whatever do you think you're doing?' screamed my mother …
- Depending on whether the characters or the setting are of particular importance, you will then introduce your characters or the setting of the story.
- To introduce your characters, swiftly identify who they are, giving some general description of their appearance and personality, and stating their relationship with each other (although you may want to reveal this later in the story). Remember, you should include only a small number of characters as there is not space in a short story to introduce too many.
- When introducing the setting and context for the story, make sure that all the key details of the part that it plays in the story are made clear.
- At this point you should introduce the key details of the plot of the story as that and the part played in it by the characters will be the main focus of your writing from this point on. As mentioned previously, a short story plot should not be too complicated, especially when first introduced, although a few complications can be introduced as the story develops.
- The main plot development in this story is that a conflict of some kind will develop between two characters or groups of characters. Remember that a conflict does not have to involve a physical fight – a conflict of wills or ideals can be more effective.
- Once the conflict has been described and developed (probably the most substantial section of your story), you should conclude the story with the resolution. This should include the outcome of the conflict and a summary of any future events resulting from it.

The points made above are listed in their most straightforward order, but you may like to experiment with changing the order in which they occur – for example, beginning with the resolution of the conflict and then flashbacks to show how it came about.

3   Write a first draft of your story.

4   Work with a partner, read one another's stories and refer back to the planning points above to offer constructive feedback.

5   Produce a final version of your story, taking in feedback and correcting any spelling and grammar errors. Choose whether to use your neatest handwriting or a computer.

7 EXPLORING COMPLEX THEMES

Reviewing

Reflect on your learning in this chapter.

Reading
- Which poem did you prefer? Why?
- How do you feel about Shakespeare's work? Do you find it easy or challenging to read? Do you enjoy it?
- What strategies have you learned for reading and understanding new words?

Speaking and listening
- How did you feel about performing *Romeo and Juliet*? Would you consider joining a performing arts group? Why or why not?
- Do you feel comfortable giving feedback to a partner? Do you find receiving feedback helpful?
- Did you work successfully as part of a group? What skills did your group use when it came to rewriting and performing *Romeo and Juliet*?

Writing
- Which aspects of the writing planning process do you find helpful or unhelpful?
- How has your story writing developed? Are there any areas you feel you could improve?

Key skills
- Pick five new words you have learned in this chapter that you found most interesting.
- Define 'pentameter'.
- What new skills have you learned that improved your writing?

Further reading
The following books, plays and poems explore complex themes:
- *The Curious Incident of the Dog in the Night-time* by Mark Haddon
- *The Book Thief* by Markus Zusak
- *The Fault in Our Stars* by John Green
- *Oranges are Not the Only Fruit* by Jeanette Winterson
- *Between Shades of Grey* by Ruta Sepetys
- *The Crossing* by Manjeet Mann
- *The New Penguin Book of Romantic Poetry* edited by Jonathan and Jessica Wordsworth

8 Bringing it all together

Vocabulary
- What are your favourite words?
- Where have you learned new words?

Speaking and listening
- What different types of sentence are there?
- What language techniques do you know?
- In what different ways can you vary your sentences?

BRINGING IT ALL TOGETHER

Reading
- When do you read for enjoyment?
- What is your favourite genre?
- What strategies do you use when reading a challenging text?

Writing
- How confident are you as a writer?
- How accurate are you as a writer?
- What decisions do you make when you write?
- Do your sentences flow, or do you build them more slowly?

LET'S TALK

This final chapter encourages you to reflect on your development in English, from the beginning of Stage 7 to the end of Stage 9.

Look at the mind map above and reflect on your personal responses, then share your reflections in a small group.

8 BRINGING IT ALL TOGETHER

Reading

Reading skills table

Look at the table below. The questions prompt you to apply the different reading skills you have developed through Stages 7 to 9.

Vocabulary and language	Grammar and punctuation
How do you work out the meaning of unfamiliar words? How has the author chosen words to suit the purpose of their text? What techniques has the author used, and how effective are they?	What range of sentence types has the writer used? Have they been used to enhance the impact? Has the writer chosen to use a formal or informal style to suit a particular purpose? Has the writer made punctuation choices in order to make an impact on the reader?
Text structure	Interpretation and analysis
Does the organisation of the text support the writer's purpose? How effective is the text organisation? Does it enhance the impact and meet the purpose?	Is the meaning clear and direct or is it hidden in different layers? What are the main themes of the text? What quotations best support your analysis?

When you are asked comprehension questions in an assessment, they have been designed to allow you to show how you have developed skills in one or more of these areas.

Activity 8.1

Working in a pair, read the text below. Take it in turns to read aloud.

Together read through the questions in Exercise 8.1. Refer to the Reading skills table above and discuss which skills will be important for each question.

Extract: 'From the Clyde to Sandy Hook' from *The Amateur Emigrant*

The wind **hauled** ahead with a **head sea**. By ten at night heavy sprays were flying and drumming over the **forecastle**; the **companion** of Steerage No. 1 had to be closed, and the door of communication through the second cabin thrown open. Either from the convenience of the opportunity, or because we had already a number of acquaintances in that part of the ship, Mr Jones and I paid it a late visit. Steerage No. 1 is shaped like an isosceles triangle,

Reading

GLOSSARY
hauled – pulled
head sea – a sea in which the waves are coming from directly ahead
forecastle – the front of a ship
companion – hatch, stairway from one deck to another
disperse – to spread over a wide area
foremost – first
forlorn – sad and lonely
pertinent – relevant
vitiated – spoiled
steerage – lower deck, with cheapest accommodation
retching – vomiting
beseeching – asking urgently
emigrant – of people leaving their own country
corporate – of a whole group
rent – torn
swath – a long area
curded – thickened
beguile – to cause to pass pleasantly
wheel-house – shelter for the wheel
wager – bet
romps – playing around
cuffed – hit
lee – side that provides shelter
deck-houses – structures on the deck
shrouds – rigging that holds the mast up
reels – lively dances

the sides opposite the equal angles bulging outward with the contour of the ship. It is lined with eight pens of sixteen bunks apiece, four bunks below and four above on either side. At night the place is lit with two lanterns, one to each table. As the steamer beat on her way among the rough billows, the light passed through violent phases of change, and was thrown to and fro and up and down with startling swiftness. You were tempted to wonder, as you looked, how so thin a glimmer could control and **disperse** such solid blackness. When Jones and I entered we found a little company of our acquaintances seated together at the triangular **foremost** table. A more **forlorn** party, in more dismal circumstances, it would be hard to imagine. The motion here in the ship's nose was very violent; the uproar of the sea often overpoweringly loud. The yellow flicker of the lantern spun round and round and tossed the shadows in masses. The air was hot, but it struck a chill from its foetor [strong smell].

From all round in the dark bunks, the scarcely human noises of the sick joined into a kind of farmyard chorus. In the midst, these five friends of mine were keeping up what heart they could in company. Singing was their refuge from discomfortable thoughts and sensations. One piped, in feeble tones, 'Oh why left I my hame [home]?' which seemed a **pertinent** question in the circumstances …

I now made my bed upon the second cabin floor, where, although I ran the risk of being stepped upon, I had a free current of air, more or less **vitiated** indeed, and running only from **steerage** to steerage, but at least not stagnant; and from this couch, as well as the usual sounds of a rough night at sea, the hateful coughing and **retching** of the sick and the sobs of children, I heard a man run wild with terror **beseeching** his friend for encouragement. 'The ship's going down!' he cried with a thrill of agony. 'The ship's going down!' he repeated, now in a blank whisper, now with his voice rising towards a sob; and his friend might reassure him, reason with him, joke at him – all was in vain, and the old cry came back, 'The ship's going down!' There was something panicky and catching in the emotion of his tones; and I saw in a clear flash what an involved and hideous tragedy was a disaster to an **emigrant** ship. If this whole parishful of people came no more to land, into how many houses would the newspaper carry woe, and what a great part of the web of our **corporate** human life would be **rent** across for ever!

The next morning when I came on deck I found a new world indeed. The wind was fair; the sun mounted into a cloudless heaven; through great dark-blue seas the ship cut a **swath** of **curded** foam. The horizon was dotted all day with companionable sails, and the sun shone pleasantly on the long, heaving deck.

We had many fine-weather diversions to **beguile** the time. There was a single chess-board and a single pack of cards. Sometimes as many as twenty of us would be playing dominoes for love … We had a regular daily competition to guess the vessel's progress; and twelve o'clock, when the result was published in the **wheel-house**, came to be a moment of considerable interest. But the interest was unmixed. Not a bet was laid upon our guesses. From the Clyde to Sandy Hook I never heard a **wager** offered or taken. We had, besides, **romps** in plenty. Puss in the Corner … was my own

8 BRINGING IT ALL TOGETHER

> favourite game; but there were many who preferred another, the humour of which was to box a person's ears until he found out who had **cuffed** him.
>
> This Tuesday morning we were all delighted with the change of weather, and in the highest possible spirits. We got in a cluster like bees, sitting between each other's feet under **lee** of the **deck-houses**. Stories and laughter went around. The children climbed about the **shrouds**. White faces appeared for the first time, and began to take on colour from the wind … Lastly, down sat the fiddler in our midst and began to discourse his **reels**, and jigs, and ballads, with now and then a voice or two to take up the air and throw in the interest of human speech.
>
> Robert Louis Stevenson

> **HINT**
> Make sure you give a **quotation** when one is asked for, otherwise it is generally better to use your own words if you can.
> - Keep the quotation short.
> - Choose the most important words and details that make the point.
> - Always put quotation marks at the beginning and end of the quotation.

> **EXTENSION**
> 1 Write a brief summary of the text.
> 2 Write a detailed analysis in response to the following question: What was Stevenson's main purpose in this text, and how effectively have his language and sentence choices been in terms of having an impact on the reader?

EXERCISE 8.1

Work alone to answer the following questions, using the skills you discussed with your partner.

1 What does the word 'pens' in paragraph 1 suggest about the state of the accommodation in steerage class? How is this reinforced by the expression 'farmyard chorus' in paragraph 2?

2 Explain, using your own words, what is meant by 'rough billows'.

3 Why does Stevenson describe the song sung in paragraph 2 as containing a 'pertinent question'?

4 From paragraph 4 (beginning 'The next morning when I came on deck …') choose three descriptive details that convey the change in mood of the weather and conditions on the voyage and explain their overall impact on the reader.

5 By referring to details of Stevenson's account explain as fully as you can the contrast between the earlier and later part of the journey.

6 Choose three expressions from Stevenson's account that suggest that it was written over 100 years ago and give reasons for your choice. Explain how the language and contextual details of Stevenson's account help you to understand the idea, experiences and values of people living in a different historical period.

> **HINT**
> When answering **summary questions**, remember to do the following:
> - Keep focused on the question when reading the passage.
> - Highlight or underline all the sections that are relevant to the question.
> - Do not write an introduction.
> - Use your own words and be as concise as possible.
> - Be especially careful in the summary to think about the question. There will always be facts in the passage that are not relevant to what you have been asked to do and part of the skill of summarising is to leave out material that is not needed. For example, if you are asked to summarise why some action would be helpful, you should not include the negative points. Doing so only wastes time and does not gain credit.

Writing

Personal response and reading for pleasure

EXERCISE 8.2

Do you have a favourite novel or short story? Do you have a favourite scene from that novel/story?

Find a passage from your favourite novel/story and write a reflective piece that:
- summarises the plot and themes of the novel/story
- explains the importance of the scene in relation to the rest of the novel/story
- analyses how the language techniques of the author has had an impact on the reader in your chosen extract.

Writing

Writing skills table

Look at the table below. The questions prompt you to apply the different writing skills you have developed through Stages 7 to 9.

Spelling, vocabulary and language	Grammar and punctuation
What strategies do you use to spell accurately? How have you chosen the words that will be effective for your piece? What techniques have you used to have an impact on your reader?	What range of sentence types will you choose to use? Why? What purpose will they serve?
Text structure	**Creation and evaluation of texts**
What did you choose as your starting point? Why? How does the text flow from beginning to end? How would you expect a reader to respond to the structure you have chosen?	What planning process will you choose? How will it help? What is the main purpose of your text? What choices could you make in order to have an impact on the reader? What viewpoint or perspective will you use? How will this support the purpose of your text? In what way will this have an impact the reader?

Writing information texts

You may find writing information texts easier than writing stories because you do not have to invent a plot, and the style is often more direct. The thing that is difficult is deciding how to organise your material. The question may give you some suggestions for what to write but you can choose whether or not to use them and should add other ideas of your own.

8 BRINGING IT ALL TOGETHER

Use your planning time, and the planning box provided, to do three things:
1. Think of enough to say and make it relevant for your audience. This sounds obvious, but you do need to spend a little time making sure you have enough material. Jot down ideas as you think of them.
2. Organise your ideas or information into groups and decide on the order in which they should appear.
3. Think about how you are going to link the sections and create an opening line for each section.

As you write out the full version, remember that you will gain credit for developing the ideas in each section beyond the opening line. It is better in the restricted time of the test to stick to three or four main ideas and develop them, rather than write down everything you can think of in a list. Try to think of at least one more thing to say about each of your ideas: an example, perhaps, or a little more detail.

Here is an example of a plan for writing an answer on the topic 'Should swimming be put on the timetable in every secondary school?'

		Should swimming be put on the timetable in every secondary school?	
1	Ideas or information to include:	**Pros** Reduces risk of drowning Healthy exercise Aids co-ordination	**Cons** Something else would have to go Not all schools have a pool Problems with students forgetting kit
2	Organise the ideas or information into groups and decide on the order:	1 Introduction – finding time for useful skills in packed curriculum 2 Pros 3 Cons 4 Conclusion – benefits outweigh problems	
3	Think of links and create an opening line for each section:	1 School is supposed to prepare students for life … 2 It is hard to imagine a subject for which there is a better case for inclusion in the curriculum than swimming … 3 Schools, however, face immediate problems when … 4 To sum up, it seems clear that …	

EXERCISE 8.3
Create a plan for writing an information text on one of these topics:
- Should children be paid for helping with the housework?
- Where would your class like to go on your next school trip and why?

Writing fiction

When students write stories, they usually do the following well:
- openings
- events
- action.

They tend to forget:
- paragraph breaks
- the importance of working towards an ending
- to keep the reader curious about what will happen next
- what the characters are thinking and feeling.

Writing

HINT
- Give insights into the minds of the characters and say what they are feeling.
- Plan an ending.
- Concentrate on using words and details that create setting, mood and character.
- In the test, you will need to spend a few minutes planning your story. It needs a beginning, middle and end. It needs characters to do things and a setting where the events happen. Remember that the question you are answering may already have given you some of these – and note that it is important to plan your ending *before* you get carried away by the middle.
- If you can think of a complete plot with a proper ending that you can write in the time of the test, that is great. But do not worry if you cannot. Look carefully at what you are asked to do. Suppose it is to describe a visit to a haunted house. You could include why you thought it was haunted, why you went, who you were with, how you got there, what the house looked like as you approached it, what made you so nervous – and end with: 'And then the door opened of its own accord.' Your piece needs a storyline running through it (in this case the journey to the house) and you should always end with some sort of climax (which you need to plan), but it does not need to be the end of the story as a whole. You will gain credit for the quality of your description and the way you build up the tension to the climax of the door opening. An approach like this can often produce a better piece of writing than trying to cram multiple twists in a plot.
- Use this outline to help you:

			Examples for 'A visit to an old house'
Basic story	1. Who the people are How many there are	A group of friends? A family? Will you write in the first person or third person?	Me and my two best friends First person
	2. Where to begin	Are you going to tell the story chronologically (from beginning to end)? Or start in the middle and use a flashback?	It all started when I saw the magazine article describing the old house in the woods. or We were halfway there when I felt something touch my shoulder. We had set out …
	3. Where to end	Real end of story or cliffhanger?	Thank goodness we all got home safely. or And then the door opened.
	4. What happens in the middle	The storyline. Make something happen that will upset the way things are – something interesting, so that readers want to see how the characters will deal with it.	Setting out from home; going the wrong way; getting lost in the woods; eventually finding the house
Filling out the details	5. Setting and atmosphere	Description and detail of place, weather, mood	Sky became very dark. Couldn't see. Trees crowded close together. House appeared suddenly through mist. Dark, gloomy, depressing.
	6. Feelings	All the same? (Some scared, some not?) Change over time? Reactions to happenings and/or atmosphere?	Tom got frightened and I tried to reassure him. But when we saw …

8 BRINGING IT ALL TOGETHER

EXERCISE 8.4

1. Try finishing this story plan. The first three rows have been filled in for you. Copy and complete the table.

A story to illustrate the importance of paying attention		
Basic story	Who	My family and me
	Beginning	We are on holiday at the seaside.
	Ending	My brother is brought back safely by rescuers.
	Storyline – what happens	
Filling it out	Description and detail	
	Feelings – mine and his	

2. Here is another story plan. This time a different two rows have been filled in for you. Copy and complete the table.

An argument that should never have happened		
Basic story	Who	
	Beginning	
	Ending	But something has changed: I have new friends, and a better attitude.
	Storyline – what happens	
Filling it out	Description and detail	
	Feelings	I realise that some of my friends are only interested in me for my looks, and that some people I never noticed before are actually quite nice.

3. Now use the table to plan a story of your own on one of these topics:
   - An unusual friendship
   - An item that goes missing

4. When you have finished your plan, write your story! Use the Hint box on the next page to help with your writing.

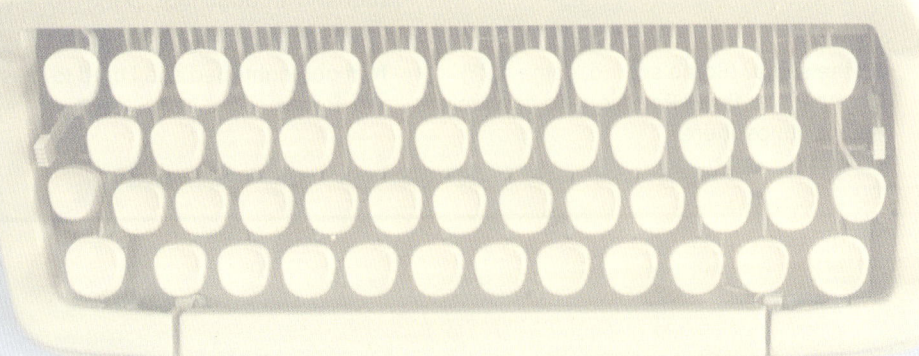

Speaking and listening

> **HINT**
> 1. *Accuracy* first! You know the mistakes you always make. Think of a way of remembering them and write it at the top of your test paper in pencil. This will remind you to check.
> 2. Learn the spellings you think you might need.
> 3. Remember to use full stops, not commas, to separate sentences.
> 4. Remember to start a new paragraph when:
>   - you start a new topic
>   - you move to a different time
>   - you shift to a new place
>   - someone else starts to speak.
> 5. Use a range of different sentence types. Try the following:
>   - Begin a sentence with an adverb ending in -ly, for example: '*Carefully*, she looked round the corner.'
>   - Embed a subordinate clause, for example: 'The man, *who had been lurking in the shadows*, sidled away.'
>   - Begin with a preposition, for example: '*Through* a gap in the fence, we could see a dog digging furiously.'
>   - Use an occasional short sentence, for example: 'It stopped.' This is especially effective if the short sentence follows a number of long ones.
> 6. Vary your vocabulary. Try to avoid very common words, such as 'nice' or 'get/got', and words that you use more in conversation with your own friends than to adults, such as 'awesome'.
> 7. Leave time to check your work. Proofread what you have written and correct any mistakes.

Speaking and listening

Speech and performance skills table

Look at the table below. These are prompts to help you think about the speech and performance skills you have developed.

Understanding	Effective group work
How will you adapt your language in order to have an impact on your listeners or audience?	What roles are needed?
How will you organise your speech or performance to make sure you are understood?	How will you explore agreements or disagreements?
How will you listen carefully and respond appropriately?	What counts as a good contribution to the group discussion?
Performance	**Evaluation**
Do you read ahead when reading aloud? Does this help with accuracy and expression?	What is a positive performance?
What will you use to help you to perform or speak clearly?	What mistakes or problems could have an impact on a performance?
What visual prompts or media will best support your speech?	How will you provide feedback that is helpful and not hurtful?

8 BRINGING IT ALL TOGETHER

Holding a debate

HINT
Try to express your ideas, even if you are not sure how to say something or if you make mistakes. Others will understand you and they can ask questions if they don't!

Activity 8.2

In a small group, read through the debate prompts below.

As a group, discuss which prompt you think would form the basis of the most interesting and important topic for debate.

Make sure that everyone in your group has a chance to voice their opinions, then decide as a group which you will choose.

Decide who will write and perform in support of or against your chosen prompt.

> A scientist makes a more valuable contribution to the world than an artist.

> Sport is fun to play and watch but it should not be taken seriously.

> We should concentrate on fairness and well-being for all people before worrying about the environment.

> Only adults should be allowed to make the rules.

Planning your speech
Plan, write, rehearse and refine your speech.
Decide how to bring your speech to life, and which language choices you will need to make.

Performance
Take it in turns for each side to deliver their speeches.
As an audience, listen and respond appropriately.

Evaluate
After the debate, write a short evaluation to feed back to different members of your group. Take into account the prompts from the speech and performance skills table.

HINT
You may be given the task of writing in favour of a belief or opinion you do not hold yourself. Being able to see the world from a different perspective is an important and advanced skill, and is also powerful personal development.

Reviewing

Reflect on your learning in this chapter.

Reading

- In what ways have your reading skills developed throughout Stages 7 to 9?
- How confident do you now feel reading aloud, and performing in front of an audience?
- What do you most enjoy reading: poetry, fiction, non-fiction? Have you discovered any new genres that you will go on to read more of?

Speaking and listening

- How have your language skills developed to enable you to express your thoughts and feelings?
- What speaking and listening skills have you developed?
- Which skills would you like to develop further?

Writing

- Do you consider yourself a writer? What are your strengths?
- Which parts of the writing process do you find more challenging?

Key skills

- List the literary devices writers use. How many can you remember from Stages 7 to 9?
- Do you enjoy studying English? What new skills have you learned?

Glossary

alliteration the repetition of consonant sounds at the beginning of words

antithesis a technique used in poetry and other forms of writing, which compares or connects opposites

assonance the use of similar sounds (particularly vowels) close together

autobiography an account of a person's life, written by the person

caesura a pause or break in the middle of a line

dash (–) used to indicate an interruption to the main structure of a sentence

descriptive writing describing a person, place, experience or thing in detail

dystopian about an imaginary state or society in which there is suffering or injustice

ellipsis (…) used to emphasise a pause; for example, to indicate uncertainty

enjambment where the end of the line is not the end of the sentence, and may not require a pause

etymology the origin of a word

exclamation mark (!) used for emphasis; for example to indicate excitement or shock

first-person narrative (using 'I') telling the story from one of the character's point of view

haiku a short poem with three lines and 17 syllables; lines 1 and 3 have five syllables each and line 2 has seven syllables

hyperbole the rhetorical technique of using exaggeration for effect

hyphen (-) used to link compound words, or to show that the rest of a word is on the next line

iambic pentameter a line of ten syllables (or five iambic feet). Each iambic foot is composed of an unstressed syllable followed by a stressed syllable

jargon words used by a profession or group that are hard to understand

memoir a true story or account of events, written from a personal point of view

metaphor an indirect comparison in which it is implied that one thing is like another, for example, *The banner of smoke flew from the factory chimney.*

morphology the study of words and parts of words such as roots, prefixes and suffixes

onomatopoeia when the sound of a word echoes its meaning, for example, *boom*

oratory the art of skilful and effective public speaking. A good orator is likely to make use of rhetoric

oxymoron a combination of words that seem to contradict each other

parentheses/brackets ( ) used to enclose supplemental information in a sentence

pathos a rhetorical and narrative technique that aims to gain the sympathy of the audience

personification giving an object or animal human characteristics

rhetoric the process of using the resources of language to persuade an audience to agree with a particular point of view

simile a direct comparison introduced by 'like' or 'as', for example, *The smoke hung from the chimney like a drooping flag.*

synonym a word that means the same as another word

voice the character and personality of the writer

Acknowledgements

Every effort has been made to trace all copyright holders, but if any have been inadvertently overlooked, the Publishers will be pleased to make the necessary arrangements at the first opportunity.

The publishers would like to thank the following for permission to reproduce copyright material:

Text credits

p.3 Jamie Crane, 'The Liechtenstein Trail: Walking the length of a country in a weekend', Nov 21, 2019, The Travel Magazine Ltd; **p.7** Anita Froneman, 'World's longest zipline to open near Caledon', 8 September 2021, Getaway; **p.8** Dervla Murphy, 'First, buy your pack animal', The Guardian, 3 January 2009, copyright Guardian News & Media Ltd 2009, www.theguardian.com/travel/2009/jan/03/dervla-murphy-travel-tips; **p.10** extract from *Neither Here nor There: Travels in Europe* by Bill Bryson (Black Swan, 1998); **pp.12–13** extract from *Himalaya* by Michael Palin, 2004, St. Martin's Press; **p.23** extract from *Memoirs: My primary school experience in Africa* by Minda Magero © reproduced by permission of Helium Inc; **pp.24–25** extract from *As I Walked Out One Midsummer Morning* by Laurie Lee, 1971, Penguin Books; **pp.28–29** extract from *Long Walk To Freedom* by Nelson Mandela, 25 April 2013, Little, Brown Book Group; **p.37** 'I, Too' by Langston Hughes; **pp.43–44** extract from *The Pillars of Hercules: A Grand Tour of the Mediterranean* by Paul Theroux, 1995, Hamish Hamilton; **pp.49–50** Coral reefs from www.oceansplasticleanup.com/Biodiversity/CoralReefs/Coral_Reefs.htm, Cleaner Oceans Foundation Ltd; **pp.51–52** 'Only Nuclear Energy Can Save the Planet' by Joshua S. Goldstein and Staffan A. Qvist, Jan 11, 2019, The Wall Street Journal; **p.60** 'The City' by Langston Hughes, © David Higham Associates Limited; **p.65** 'February Evening in New York' by Denise Levertov, from *Collected Earlier Poems 1940 -1960*. Copyright © 1957, 1958, 1959, 1960, 1961, 1979 by Denise Levertov. Reprinted with the permission of New Directions Publishing Corporation, www.wwnorton.com/nd/welcome.htm; **pp.67–68** extract from 'Games at Twilight' from *Games at Twilight* by Anita Desai (William Heinemann, 1978) © 1978 Anita Desai, reproduced by permission of the author c/o Rogers, Coleridge & White Ltd, 20 Powis Mews, London W11 1JN; **p.71** 'Cat-rap' by Grace Nichols from *The Poet Cat* © Curtis Brown; **p.91** 'Education is the only solution' by Malala Yousafzai; **pp.98–99** extract from *Tears of the Giraffe* by Alexander McCall Smith, (Abacus, 2003); **pp.104–108** 'The Pedestrian' by Ray Bradbury, 1951, published in *The Golden Apples of the Sun* by Ray Bradbury, Heinemann Educational Publishers; 1st New edition 1990; **p.115** 'Not Waving but Drowning' by Stevie Smith from *Collected Poems of Stevie Smith*. Copyright © 1972 by Stevie Smith

Photo credits

p.1 © Reichdernatur/stock.adobe.com; **p.3** © Dziewul/stock.adobe.com; **p.6** © Kaspars Grinvalds/stock.adobe.com; **p.7** © Ammit/stock.adobe.com; **p.8** © Eamonn McCabe/Popperfoto/Getty Images; **p.10** © Mhgstan/stock.adobe.com; **p.11** © John Swannell; **p.12** © Milosz Maslanka/stock.adobe.com; **p.14** © Natty/stock.adobe.com; **p.16** © Michael Rosskothen/stock.adobe.com; **p.19** © Leonid Andronov/stock.adobe.com; **p.21** © Fyle/stock.adobe.com; **p.23** © nadezhda1906/stock.adobe.com; **p.24** © Keith Waldegrave/Mail On Sunday/Shutterstock; **p.28** © Alessia Pierdomenico/Shutterstock.com; **p.31** © Evenfh/stock.adobe.com; **p.34** *t* © STR/AFP/Getty Images, *b* © Featureflash Photo Agency/Shutterstock.com; **p.36** © Library of Congress Prints and Photographs Division Washington, D.C. 20540 USA [LC-USZ62-43605]; **p.41** © Imagenatural/stock.adobe.com; **p.42** © Pe3check/stock.adobe.com; **p.49** © Tunatura/stock.adobe.com; **p.52** © Marlee/stock.adobe.com; **p.53** © Bptu/stock.adobe.com; **p.59** © Diversepixel/stock.adobe.com; **p.61** *t* © Tanyakim/stock.adobe.com, *b* © Pelooyen/stock.adobe.com; **p.63** *t* © Pictorial Press Ltd/Alamy Stock Photo, *b* © Stephen/stock.adobe.com; **p.64** © Chris Felver/Premium Archive/Getty Images; **p.65** © Deberarr/stock.adobe.com; **p.66** © Raphael Gaillarde/Gamma-Rapho/Getty Images; **p.70** *t* © Onephoto/stock.adobe.com, *b* © Stuart Clarke/Shutterstock; **p.72** © Granger/Shutterstock; **p.75** © Oneinchpunch/stock.adobe.com; **p.77** © Lynea/stock.adobe.com; **pp.78, 124** © Ladychelyabinsk/stock.adobe.com; **p.79** © DC Studio/stock.adobe.com; **p.81** © phaisarnwong2517/stock.adobe.com; **p.84** © Tom Wang/stock.adobe.com; **p.87** © Lithiumphoto/stock.adobe.com; **p.91** © Andrew Gombert/EPA European Press Photo b.v./Alamy Stock Photo; **p.93** © Siraanamwong/stock.adobe.com; **p.94** © Jemastock/stock.adobe.com; **p.95** © Jemastock/stock.adobe.com; **p.97** © Baker Street Scans/Alamy Stock Photo; **p.104** © MediaPunch Inc/Alamy Stock Photo; **p.105** © Ilya Nikolaevic/stock.adobe.com; **p.111** © BrunoBarillari/stock.adobe.com; **p.112** *t* © Artur Nyk/stock.adobe.com, *b* © Stock Montage/Archive Photos/Getty Images; **p.115** © Evening Standard/Hulton Archive/Getty Images; **p.119** © Alastair Muir/Shutterstock; **p.120** © Landmark Media/Alamy Stock Photo; **p.127** © Iren Moroz/stock.adobe.com; **p.131** © Monticelllllo/stock.adobe.com; **pp.134–5** © Pixelbliss/stock.adobe.com

t = top, *b* = bottom, *m* = middle, *l* = left, *r* = right